Another Look at Atlantis

AND FIFTEEN OTHER ESSAYS

Books by Willy Ley

ANOTHER LOOK AT ATLANTIS
AND FIFTEEN OTHER ESSAYS

FOR YOUR INFORMATION

ROCKETS, MISSILES AND MEN IN SPACE

WATCHERS OF THE SKY

ENGINEER'S DREAMS

EXOTIC ZOOLOGY

THE CONQUEST OF SPACE

THE EXPLORATION OF MARS
(with Wernher von Braun)

BEYOND THE SOLAR SYSTEM

DAWN OF ZOOLOGY

DISCOVERY OF THE ELEMENTS

MISSILES, MOONPROBES AND MEGAPARSECS

RANGER TO THE MOON

MARINER TO MARS

THE BORDERS OF MATHEMATICS

ON EARTH AND IN THE SKY

TRANSLATIONS:

THE MOON CAR

OTTO HAHN,
A SCIENTIFIC AUTOBIOGRAPHY

Another Look at Atlantis

AND FIFTEEN OTHER ESSAYS
BY WILLY LEY

BELL PUBLISHING COMPANY
NEW YORK

Contents

Introduction

Willy Ley can only be described as an Ologist. To add any prefix which might restrict the meaning of that term would be grossly unjust. He was educated as a zoologist and holds an Honorary Doctorate from Adelphi University, but his interests range from agriology to zymology, and he has written with rare knowledge and charm about almost every field of human learning.

When I first met him, nearly thirty years ago, he had only recently fled from Germany in horror at the Nazi policies. At that time, he was a pleasantly bearlike man with a thick German accent—and with one of the largest and subtlest English vocabularies I have ever encountered. The discussion, as I remember it, rambled from the technical aspects of photochemistry to the history of the last Ice Age, with side trails into multilingual humor and the ethics of head hunting.

Rockets were never mentioned, which seems strange. Willy was already *the* authority on the subject. He had discovered and popularized Oberth's theoretical work on space travel and had helped to organize the German Rocket Society which led directly to the later work of men like Wernher von Braun. Most science fiction writing depended heavily on him for the facts on space travel.

Since then, his reputation in that field has become world wide. Through many editions and under various titles, his book on *Rockets, Missiles and Space Travel* has been the

viii

Introduction

textbook for a generation of space scientists, while other readers have been enlightened and delighted by a host of his more popular articles and books. More than any other man, he has prepared the world for the Space Age which he helped to create.

All this has been accomplished without any neglect of his other interests. *Galaxy Science Fiction* was astute enough to have him do a regular column, *For Your Information*. For nearly two decades he has appeared there with facts and insights on everything from animals that shouldn't exist to mythology that just might be based on fact. Few magazine columns have endured so long, and none has ever ranged so freely across all fields or won a more loyal host of readers. The examples in this book are selected—but typical of what can be expected of his work.

The last time I met Willy was a couple of months ago. His hair has become a bit gray and his accent a trifle less noticeable, but he seems unchanged otherwise by time. I had been telling of my reaction to the pianistic artistry of Eugen d'Albert as preserved on the marvelous Welte piano rolls. When I finished, Willy put down his glass of vodka and launched enthusiastically into the life and times of d'Albert and the concert world of 1900.

I hadn't known that Willy Ley was a musicologist, but I wasn't surprised. As I said, the man is the world's only qualified Ologist.

Lester del Rey
Managing Editor
Galaxy Publishing Corporation

Another Look at Atlantis

AND FIFTEEN OTHER ESSAYS

Another Look at Atlantis

THIS IS A STORY I was told some thirty-five years ago by a novelist who swore that it actually happened. It concerned another writer whom both of us knew and who wrote a great deal for a weekly family magazine. One day the editor of that magazine, after an evening of spirited discussion with his wife and her two sisters, asked him to write a definitive article on Atlantis. If necessary, it could be a series of articles, but they should be *definitive*, clearing up the whole problem once and for all time!

The writer, whose knowledge of Atlantis was about equal to that of any other educated man who has not made a special study of the subject, phoned a librarian he knew and told him (this was in Europe, where librarians are usually male) that he had to read up on Atlantis and would be over the following morning. Would the librarian be so good and assemble the most important books for him?

When he arrived at the library there was a desk reserved for him, and it was piled high with books. The librarian explained that these were the most recent works and a few important older ones. And there was a paperbound sheaf of mimeographed pages. This was what the librarian called "a reasonably complete bibliography"—of about 1700 titles. After his friend had finished with the books he had pulled out, he might wish to check through the bibliography and mark what else he wanted to read. The library would not have all of these titles, of course, but a few score of them probably could be turned up.

I don't know what happened to that "definitive" article—chances are it was never written.

However, other people who did not feel beaten down by the volume of earlier literature kept writing books on Atlantis. As has been the case in the past, they ranged over the whole spectrum from "inner visions" to sober attempts to find an interpretation that satisfied both historical tradition and recognized facts. My reason for bringing up the nearly-talked-to-death Atlantis theme once more is that something very unusual has taken place in recent years: there are a few new facts!

No, it is not yet the "definitive" story that magazine editor wanted so desperately. For the core of the Atlantis problem is that the "definitive" solution involves an impossibility—namely that of reading the mind of a man who died over 2300 years ago.

I mean, of course, Plato, who lived from about 427 B.C. to 347 B.C.

Atlantis is mentioned in two of his works, the two "dialogues" ("discussions" would be a better label) *Timaios* and *Kritias*. They are the only, repeat, *only* sources. Every other mention of Atlantis is based on these writings of Plato. There are *no* independent sources.

Nor did Plato claim to have any direct and personal knowledge. He had one of his characters quote Solon, a historical figure (*ca.* 638 B.C. to 559 B.C.), who was Archon of Athens (beginning in 594 B.C.) and who is known to have traveled extensively. So the true and again only source of the Atlantis story, if we accept Plato's word, is Solon. Please note that Solon was dead for 150 years when Plato was a young man; it is precisely as if a young man of our time told of something that, through family tradition, goes back to George Washington.

I just said that the original source was Solon *if* we accept
Plato's statements. As for that there can be only two opinions: we can either believe that Plato wrote down what Solon
originally said (admitting that Plato's version might not be
an absolutely accurate rendering) or else we can believe that
it was a fable invented for the purpose of providing a setting
for Plato's "ideal state."

Aristotle, Plato's pupil, was convinced that Atlantis had
been invented for philosophizing purposes. The Roman Pliny
the Elder, four centuries later, just burdened Plato with the
responsibility, sounding somewhat petulant, possibly because
in all his omnivorous reading he had never found another
source. The picture is the same with all the authors of the
classical period: they either took Atlantis to be a "philosophical parable" or else just wrote "according to Plato." Nobody got excited one way or the other.

After the interval of one and a half millenia, when nobody
had the time or inclination to think about such problems, a
surprising number of learned men decided that Atlantis must
have been based on a dim knowledge of the existence of a
continent on the other side of the ocean. The Spanish historian Francisco Lopez de Gomara (1510-1560) was the first
to say that America must have been meant. Sir Francis Bacon
(1561-1626) said the same, and the German educator Janus
Joannes Bircherod even coined the sentence *orbe novo non
novo* ("the New World is not new") in 1663. These thoughts
were still echoed two centuries later by the great Alexander
von Humboldt.

The first man to have accepted the story as literally true
seems to have been the learned and versatile Jesuit Father
Athanasius Kircher (1601-1680), who invented the magic
lantern and thought that he had deciphered hieroglyphic
writing. He pictured Atlantis as a small continent in the Atlantic Ocean. (Fig. 1.). Though he said in his book that the
island is pictured in precise agreement with Plato's descrip-

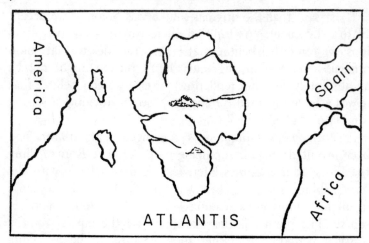

Fig. 1. *Atlantis according to Kircher. From his book* Mondus subter-
raneus (1644). *This tracing has been inverted, in the original north
is at the bottom.*

tion this is not really so, as we'll see. All that can be said in
favor of it is that the small continent is about the size stated
by Plato, that it has a mountain and several large rivers.

But before we go on it seems to be practical to see what
Plato actually said. The information provided in the *Timaios*,
the earlier of the two dialogues, is relatively meager. The man
who tells about Atlantis in both dialogues is one Kritias,
grandson of a man by the same name, who was a son of
Dropides, who was a personal friend of Solon. Solon, Kritias
the Younger, reports, traveled to Egypt; the actual and historical date for that trip is somewhere between 590 B.C. and
580 B.C. He went to the city of Sais and had long conversa-
tions with the priests there, who told him that their goddess
Neith, whom the Greeks call Athena, had founded both cities, Sais 8000 years ago and Athens 9000 years ago. At that
time there existed an island beyond the pillars of Hercules:
"it was larger than Lybia and Asia put together."

This last sentence needs two emendations. One is that "Asia" means what we call Asia minor, and the other is that the original Greek sentence contains a word that cannot be translated by just one other word. That word is *meizon*. The customary translation is "larger" in the meaning of "greater in extent." But the word can also mean "more powerful," and since the story then goes on to talk about an invasion from Atlantis this translation sounds more likely. The priests said that this invasion had the purpose of subjugating the eastern portion of the Mediterranean and that they almost succeeded but were finally beaten by the Athenians. "Afterwards there occurred violent earthquakes and floods and in a single day and night of rain your warlike men in a body sank into the earth, and the island of Atlantis in a like manner disappeared and was sunk beneath the sea."

There is no more about Atlantis in the *Timaios*, and if the other dialogue which is named after Kritias did not exist, nobody would have paid much attention to the ancient invasion and ancient catastrophe. Everybody would have accepted Aristotle's commentary: "He who invented it [namely Atlantis] also destroyed it."

But it was the *Kritias* that excited everybody, because here the narrator went into detail. On the island in question there dwelled people, and Poseidon fell in love with one of the girls. He lived with her on a small mountain and begat five pairs of twins, all male and all future kings. He surrounded the mountain with several circular courses of water "so that no man could get to the island for ships and voyages were not yet heard of." That these concentric courses of water were made by a god must be taken to mean that this was a natural formation. But the later kings, after the population had become numerous, embellished on this formation with walls and canals through the circular courses of land, so that ships could pass from one into the other. The water courses were spanned by a bridge which, of course, had to have three sections. (This explains why the word "bridge" is used in the singular, though three bridges are involved.)

The plan of the finished city is shown in Fig. 2. The cen-

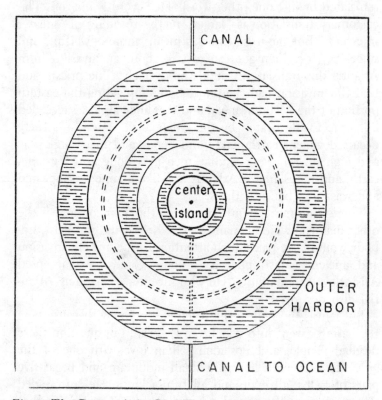

Fig. 2. *The Center of the City. This is a scale drawing of the center section of the city, as described by Plato. The broken circle indicates the race course.*

tral island, with the stele inscribed with the laws, a temple of Poseidon and the king's palace, had a diameter of 5 stadia*.

* A stadion was divided into 600 feet, Greek. Its length is now taken to have been 185 meters, or 607 feet, U.S. measure. The secondary meaning—of "race course"—of this word is derived from the fact that the race course at Olympia was one stadion in length.

The innermost circular water course was one stadion in width, and the land circle around it had a width of two stadia. Then followed a water circle with a width of two stadia, also called the Inner Harbor; a circle of land, holding a "hippodrome" or circle course for race horses with a width of three stadia came next, surrounded by a water course, the Outer Harbor, of a width of three stadia.

A straight canal, half a stadion in width and one and a half stadia in depth, stretched from the Outer Harbor to the ocean. It was fifty stadia long, so that the distance from the center of the island to the shore was 63½ stadia. At that distance a high circular wall was built that went all around the city; on the side away from the ocean it touched the Grand Canal. The Grand Canal was 10,000 stadia in length, forming a rectangle of 2000 by 3000 stadia. The area was divided into 600 squares by irrigation ditches, each 100 feet in width. (Fig. 3.)

The overall idea seems to have been that several rivers emptying into the Grand Canal would keep it full of water and fill the irrigation ditches, with the overflow going into the circular Outer Harbor and, finally, through the fifty-stadia canal into the ocean. A modern hydraulics engineer would be quite unhappy with such an open system lacking all locks. Two years of drought in the interior, and ocean water would storm in, going the other way and ruining all crops. But let's not quibble here but go on. The total area—the irrigated plain, the city itself and the space between the irrigated plain and the seashore—would measure 3000 by 2127 stadia, or close to 6.4 million square stadia, approximately 77,600 square miles. Since there were ten kingdoms on the island—assuming that they were all the same size, which is not stated anywhere explicitly—the total area of the island should have been about 800,000 square miles, roughly three times the size of Texas.

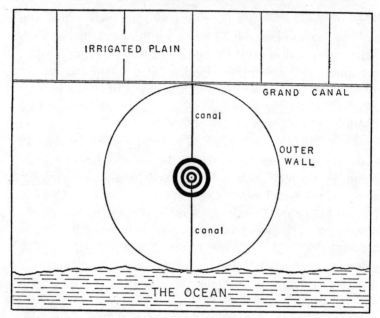

Fig. 3. Overall plan of the City.

Even this condensed retelling shows that there is an enormous difference between the two Atlantis narratives in Plato's work. The *Timaios*, with its recital about an invasion and military engagements terminated by a natural catastrophe, does convey the impression that an older tale is here merely retold. But the *Kritias*, with its enormous elaboration of arrangements and dimensions, plus such detail as the color of the stones in the various walls and the kinds of metal used for ornamentation and reinforcement, is obviously the result of much pondering about what an outstanding city, originally conceived by a god and embellished by godlike kings should be like.

The "searchers for Atlantis," who accepted the story word for word, wall for wall and water course for water course, faced one major handicap, namely the great size. It prompted

those who did not dare to doubt to look in all kinds of unlikely places. In sequence, southern Sweden, the Caucasus
mountains, South America, Ceylon, Algiers and the western
bulge of Africa were acclaimed as the place where Atlantis
must have been—not withstanding the minor fact that all of
them are still in existence well above sea level. And, of course,
there was no trace of anything that could possibly date back
to 9600 B.C.

Could something be wrong with the figures themselves?

More than one scholar has guessed at a confusion between
solar years and periods of the moon. If the Egyptians spoke
in terms of "moons" (of 30 days each) then 9000 "years"
would shrink to 742 actual years. Since Solon heard the tale
in about 590 B.C., the date would become 1332 B.C., a far
more believable figure. But there is another possibility for a
mistake. It is said in so many words in the *Kritias* that the
Egyptian records had been translated into Egyptian from another language—it is not stated which one. Solon then translated them into Greek, and he may have taken the Egyptian
written symbol for "100" to mean "1000." In that case the
invasion would date 900 years before Solon's visit or about
1500 B.C., while the rectangular plain enclosed by the Grand
Canal would measure 200 by 300 stadia or 23 by 34½ miles.
The city itself would remain the same size, because all the
figures involved are smaller than "100."*

The suggestion that the problem had been made intracta-
ble by such a simple mistake in translation was made by the
seismologist Professor Anghelos Galanapoulos. Since Prof.
Galanapoulos is Greek, he is thoroughly acquainted with all
the Greek legends and with everything by and about Plato.
And Prof. Galanapoulos has been thinking about Atlantis for
a long time.

* This assumes, of course, that the plan of the city was a part of Solon's
tale; most modern commentators have strong doubts about that.

Under 36½° northern latitude and 25½° eastern longitude in the blue Aegaean Sea there lies a small group of islands, collectively known as the Santorini group. It consists of two large islands, Thera and Therasia, and a few small ones, namely Aspronisi ("white island") and three with names that have the word *kameni* ("burning") in common. They are Palaia Kameni, Nea Kameni and Mikra Kameni, the "old burning island," the new one and the tiny one. They are all volcanic. In 1866 there was a long-lasting eruption that was carefully investigated by a French scientist named Fouque. With the aid of data furnished by Fouque, Professor Melchior Neumayr of the University of Vienna drew up a table of known eruptions.

There had been one in 198 B.C., during which the island of Palaia Kameni came into existence. Another eruption in 726 A.D. enlarged this island. In 1573 Mikra Kameni was formed. In 1650 there was another eruption that produced only minor changes, but in 1707 there began one that lasted five years, with Nea Kameni as the result. And the one in 1866 formed an island that was named Georgios Island but soon combined with Nea Kameni.

In, say, 250 B.C. the Santorini group consisted of Thera and Therasia only; in 1890 it looked as shown in Fig. 4.

To the geologists of the latter part of the nineteenth century the shapes of Thera and Therasia suggested that they were remaining pieces of a former volcano that had covered the whole area of the Santorini group and that had blown up at some time in the past. Since the eastern Mediterranean is an area of early literacy, but since no classical record made any mention of such a catastrophe, the great eruption must have taken place before writing, say before 1000 B.C. The explosion of Krakatoa in the Sunda Sea, that took place in late August of 1883 and threw a cubic mile of pumice and other volcanic ejecta into the atmosphere, came just in time to demonstrate what a volcano could do. The catastrophe

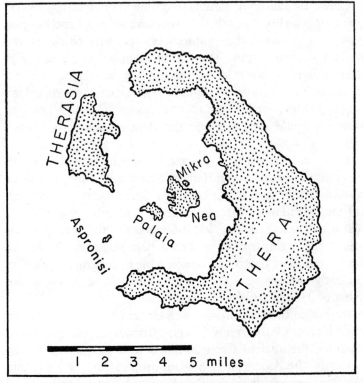

Fig. 4. The Santorini group in the Aegaean Sea.

that left Thera and Therasia must have been of the type of the Krakatoa explosion, and probably even bigger and more violent.

Of course, Thera and Therasia are covered with thick layers of pumice and volcanic ashes. It probably would never have occurred to anybody to start excavations to see whether anything could be found underneath these layers. If the thought *had* occurred to anybody, it is doubtful whether money for such a project could have been found. But science was aided by a commercial venture at this point.

Greek businessmen "mined" the pumice for making ce-
ment that was needed on the mainland for construction purposes. And under the pumice and ashes remains of old
buildings were found! Household utensils of shaped clay
were recovered. No trace of inscriptions was found and virtually no metallic objects. But Fouque described two golden
rings, implying trade since there is no gold locally. Too bad
that one could only guess at the date of this early inhabi-
tation.

I have to admit that I do not know who was the first to
connect the ancient eruption of Santorini with the end of
the Minoan culture on Crete. Early Crete had an astonishing
culture, with large cities and enormous temples, and it was a
maritime power. As knowledge about ancient Crete grew, its
role as the dominant sea power in the eastern Mediterranean
became so clear that some scholars began to wonder whether
the early Cretans were not the model for the sea-going Phaia-
kians of Homer's *Odyssey*.

And since there are many resemblances between the sailors
from Homer's Scheria and Plato's Atlanteans, and since both
resemble the ancient Cretans, it has been suggested at least
twice—by the American E. S. Balch in 1921 and the German
W. Brandenstein in 1952—that Plato's Atlantis was mainly a
poetic memory of the Cretans.

Legends, poetry, speculation and philosophy aside, there
was a very real mystery about the end of the Minoan culture
on Crete. Before about 1400 B.C. there were large cities, but
some time after that date there were only small rural settle-
ments. And most of the archeologists who tried to reconstruct
life during the Minoan culture slowly became convinced that
there was a sudden "event" that marked the beginning of the
change. In places it looked as if artisans had dropped their
tools in the middle of their normal activities and run away.
The most obvious explanation was that there had been a
sudden call to arms to ward off an invasion. It sounded simple

Fig. 5. The area covered by volcanic ash from the eruption of 1500 B.C.

and also sounded logical, but there were difficulties. A would-be invader would first have been engaged by the large Cretan fleet, so that a sudden call to arms was not too likely. Besides, who could have invaded Crete?

It was an event, all right. But the event was the eruption of Santorini—which is now estimated to have thrown about four times the volume of pumice and cinders into the atmosphere as Krakatoa did in 1883. While the sudden appearance of enormous black clouds must have been frightening, the fall of cinders and ashes at such a distance could not have been too serious. But such an eruption of an island volcano produces an enormous tidal wave. The one caused by the Krakatoa explosion drowned over 36,000 people on the neighboring islands. The wave from the Santorini explosion must have smashed the whole Cretan fleet, probably assembled along the north shore of the island. It killed an unknown number of Cretans, and it caused the end of the Minoan culture, eliminating it much faster and more thoroughly than any invasion by human enemies would have done.

The effects of the distant volcanic eruption were felt as far away as Egypt, though in Egypt the effects were psychological —darkness for a period of time—rather than physical.

So here we have, in the right area and fairly closely at the right time, the great natural catastrophe of which Solon spoke. And it fits the general picture: the Greeks would have learned about it from the Egyptians. The Egyptians could also have told Solon about invasions from the West. We know that there were such invasions by what the Egyptians call the "sea people." Actually these invasions took place about 250 years after the Santorini catastrophe; but, since all this was told to Solon another 600 years later, the Egyptians may have confused the sequence of events. Or else Solon did not understand too well what they said. Or else Plato thought that it would make a better story if a human invasion was terminated by a natural catastrophe.

The new knowledge about the approximate date of the Santorini catastrophe as the reason for the end of the Minoan culture on Crete has certainly shed new light on the "sources" of the Atlantis story. It does seem more likely now that Solon actually brought the tale from Egypt and the manuscript of the older *Kritias*—believed by most scholars to have been Plato's literary invention—might have existed.

But Professor Galanopoulos went one step farther. Knowing, from personal observation, that Santorini was inhabited before the catastrophe, he has superimposed the scale map

of Plato's city on the map of the Santorini group. He found
that the whole group would fit inside the Outer Wall of
Plato's city and that the city itself would fit into the space
between Thera and Therasia. As any one of my readers can
try for himself, there is such a fit, though a rather poor one.

Personally I consider the similarity in size just a coincidence. I don't think that Santorini *was* Atlantis . . . though
there can hardly be any doubt that Santorini was the main
cause of the Atlantis story.

2

The Wreck of *La Lutine*

IT WAS THE YEAR VIII of the French Republic, and all of Europe (where the same year was called 1799 A.D.) was trying to recover from the wars they had fought against this republic. Italy had been overwhelmed by the French. The areas now known as Belgium and the Netherlands were ruled by the French too and Prussia and Austria, as well as Spain, had been forced to sign peace treaties they did not like at all.

The only major power in western Europe that had not been defeated was Great Britain. In fact, in some respects it was better off in the "Year VIII" than it had been when the French Republic had been founded. The British fleet had defeated the French whenever they met, Great Britain's colonial possessions had grown by annexing former French colonies and, while the French had fought battles all over the map of Europe, the British had extended their trade and achieved general prosperity.

One other place was prosperous too, the independent seaport of Hamburg.

Hamburg had been a seaport ever since it had been founded. While it had never been poverty stricken, it had not become important until (and because of) the American Revolutionary War. Some quirk of commercial fate had channelled lots of trade through Hamburg because the Thirteen Colonies wanted to be independent. The many wars against revolutionary France had brought additional trade to Hamburg and while Hamburg's commercial interests had been opposed to those of Great Britain in 1776 and for a few years after, both now pulled the same commercial rope.

Hamburg got all the trade that would have gone to Holland under normal conditions. But there was a problem: the available cash did not match the increase of the trade volume.

It is reported that the banks had to charge an interest rate of 30 per cent for loans, which was about equal to the profits the merchants would have made if they had had enough cash on hand. But the sea captains that carried the merchandise—most of them Scandinavians—wanted to be paid. And while the local banks could get almost any interest rate they charged, they were handicapped by lack of cash too. Logically the merchants of Hamburg sent out a cry for help to the bankers of London. And the latter were only too pleased to help; it was a clear-cut case of one hand washing the other.

The London bankers, in a very short time, got the sum of 24 million dollars together. Most of it was in gold coins, the remainder consisted of bars of gold and silver which the City of Hamburg could use to mint their own coin. The problem was to get the treasure to Hamburg.

While there was no longer a French fleet there were still French ships prowling the North Sea and the Channel. A commercial vessel traveling under military escort would only attract attention. The Londoners decided on using a vessel which they had captured from the French a few years earlier. It was a fast-sailing and heavily armed warship named *La Lutine*—the English had not even bothered to change the name. The gold and silver were quietly loaded in barrels and boxes which did not betray their contents by their appearance. The cargo might as well have been so many barrels of salted herring and boxes of soap.

La Lutine carried the unusually large crew of 300 men, many of them armed to repel a possible enemy attack. She was ready to sail early in October 1799. The captain waited for a few days for good weather and cast off a few hours after sunset on October 9th.

The weather was good, the wind was favorable and by midnight the ship—which had sailed from Yarmouth, the easternmost point of England—had covered more than half the distance. But then a strong storm came from the northeast, blowing in the direction of Holland.

Several hours later the storm-blown ship reached the string of islands to the north of Holland—presumably its original coastline—and ran aground near the island of Terschelling. *La Lutine* capsized immediately and sank. Only two of its large crew survived.

The merchants of Hamburg must have managed somehow to survive their financial crisis. The merchants and bankers of London quietly approached Lloyd's of London, which had insured vessel and cargo, and collected. And the two surviving sailors spread the tale of the gold.

The government of the Batavian Republic—which was the name of Holland at the moment—acted promptly by declaring that the treasure on board the sunken vessel was government property. But that is the only action the government took; for some reason nobody was in a hurry.

Two years later an order was issued to try and salvage the money. This order went to the local authorities and they ascertained that the wreck was accessible at low tide. Hence local fishermen were sworn in and told to see what they could do. The fishermen went to work with oyster forks and long-handled nets and succeeded in extracting about a million dollars worth of gold bars and coins during the summer and fall of 1801. But during the winter 1801-02 currents shifted and in the spring of 1802 *La Lutine* was no longer visible. In fact she had been covered up with a layer of sand estimated to have been 50 or 60 feet in thickness.

In 1814 Napoleon was finally defeated. Peace was established and with it a new Kingdom of the Netherlands, ruled

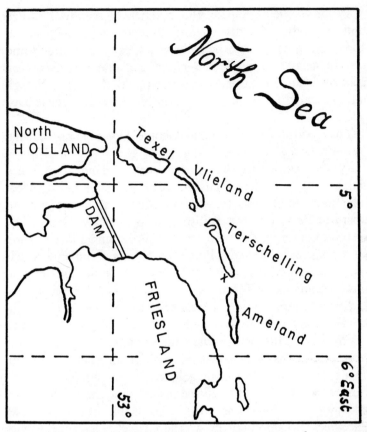

Fig. 6. X *marks the spot, as usual, in this case a spot where twenty
million dollars in gold are waiting for skilled and ingenious rescuers.*

by Willem Frederik of Orange who called himself Willem I.
Of course he knew the story of *La Lutine* but seems to have
been convinced all along that salvage was impossible. When
approached by a group of Dutch merchants and bankers in
1821 he chartered a "Privileged Salvage Company" without
hesitation, merely stipulating that one half of everything recovered was to be handed over to the crown.

While the new company sent experienced men to Terschelling to study the situation and to make recommendations about the procedure to be followed, Lloyd's of London and the financial community felt glum. The war was over. The gold on board *La Lutine* was British gold. And even though it was located in Dutch waters they had hoped to get it back one day.

They petitioned their king—George IV—who approached Willem I.

Willem wanted to show that he was England's friend and did not really believe that the treasure could be salvaged. The thing to do was to issue an edict that the money on board of *La Lutine* was British Crown Property. George IV, in turn, conferred the property to Lloyd's, and Lloyd's made an arrangement with the Privileged Salvage Company which now represented British interests. But the signing of the various documents was the only thing that did happen; *La Lutine* was buried under a layer of sand that seemed to grow thicker every year.

From 1823, the year the transfer of the property had taken place, until 1857 nothing happened at all. The "asset" of about 23 million dollars in gold could not be approached. But in 1857 the currents shifted again. Now the sea began to take away the sand it had piled up for half a century. In 1858 the wreck became actually accessible and men wearing the newly invented diving suits went to work.

They happened to have access to the place where the gold bars had been stored, and within three months they recovered half a million dollars worth. But then came the winter and a new shift of currents. In Spring 1859 the wreck was covered with sand again, but the layer was only a few feet thick and the divers thought that they could continue, at least in a few places around the wreck. For a while they were right. During 1859 and 1860 they recovered another one and a half million dollars worth of gold. But the sand layer grew in thickness and by the end of 1860 the work was discontinued.

But this was also the time when a new profession, the engineer, was in the ascendancy. Engineers are naturally of the opinion that obstacles can be overcome by good engineering. After all, they had invented a workable diving suit and meanwhile they had also invented dredging devices with buckets on endless chains. Such "digging ladders" as they were called, steam-powered, of course, should be able to do the job. The mechanical diggers would remove the sand and then the divers would be able to do the fine work and remove the gold.

Operation Steam Dredge got underway in 1866.

The concept had been correct, it was merely a case of the currents being stronger. Also the currents worked twenty-four hours a day all year round, while the dredging operation worked only in summer and in good weather. The result of *seven years* of work consisted of 20,000 dollars in gold coins.

It was disheartening and the only solace consisted in the sure knowledge that the treasure was there. The Privileged Salvage Company did not chase a rumor that might or might not be true, it just battled difficulties that might diminish again. And, after all, the engineers built new machines all the time. At some time better machinery and better conditions would come together.

Every year a new attempt was made but the success was negligible; the salvaged precious metal paid only a few per cent of the cost. In 1900 the company declared officially that it no longer considered the venture possible and asked to be released from its contract.

The financial circles of London remained optimistic, and one can hardly differ.

It was a fact that there were over 20 million dollars in gold left in the wreck. The depth of the water was virtually negligible, any good diver could put in three to four hours of work at that depth. The sand was the only problem and where the

digging ladders had failed suction pumps ought to be successful.

A firm specializing in such work, the "National Salvage
Association", felt certain of both its financial strength and its
engineering ability and offered a contract to Lloyd's and to
the Dutch Company. It said, in substance, that the National
Salvage Association would salvage the treasure of *La Lutine*
at its own expense and would keep 70 per cent of the gold
recovered, 15 per cent would go to Lloyd's and 15 per cent
to the Dutch group.

Since the Dutch group had given up hope, even 15 per cent
was a windfall, it would mean three million dollars if the
British actually recovered the treasure. The managers of
Lloyd's reasoned the same way and both signed the contract.

The National Salvage Association did not waste money on
trying what had been tried before. It was ridiculous that divers spend time under water trying to pick out single coins
from the sand. The job of the divers was obviously to guide
the machinery that would do all the actual work.

An available steamship was adapted for the specific job of
recovering *La Lutine's* gold. A large wire-mesh cage was built
at the stern of the salvage vessel, overhanging the stern for a
distance of about 15 feet. A large pipe that could be lengthened or shortened and that had a diameter of about two feet,
was attached amidships. Underwater electric lamps were
hanging from cables to provide illumination for the divers,
and hooks and grapples also hung overboard so that the divers could attach heavy objects—say a money barrel that was
still intact—to be hoisted aboard. (A few gun barrels, an an-
chor and the ship's bell were salvaged that way.) But the
main plan of action relied on the pipe which was connected
with a powerful suction pump. The water and sand sucked
up through that pipe was conveyed into the wire-mesh cage
at the stern of the vessel. The water and the sand would
thereby be discharged into the sea, but anything else, espe-

cially loose coins, would stay in the cage, to be collected at intervals. It was all very carefully thought out: the suction pump would gradually "excavate" the wreck so that the divers could go to work in the ship's interior and all incidental salvage was purely mechanical.

The work began in 1911 and everything looked promising.

There had been only one unknown factor and that was the amount of sand that the current would deposit on and around the wreck. It turned out that the current carried more sand per hour than the suction pump could remove.

Well, if the current was the real culprit there was still another way. One could change the path of the current and one did not even need new equipment.

If a channel at the bottom of the shallow sea provided a short cut for the flow of the current, no new sand would be deposited on the wreck. It was even possible that some sand would be removed. After carefully checking the path of the current and studying all the associated problems the solution emerged.

It would need a channel running in a certain direction which had to be slightly over 6000 feet long. The channel would also have to be fairly deep, so that the total amount of sand to be moved would be about 1½ million tons. But the suction pump on board the salvage vessel could handle the job, if given time.

Unfortunately the weather was generally bad in the area all through 1912 so that the total number of hours during which the vessel could work was just about 300. But in the spring of 1913 the job was finished and all the calculations had been proved correct.

After the channel had been finished the wreck of *La Lutine* could be exposed quickly. By July 1913 the midship section was accessible and the divers reported that there was a gap in the hull. It was too small to enter but the divers could reach in and feel around and they were sure that they felt stacked bars of metal. The next step was, obviously, that the gap had to be widened so that the divers would be able to enter the hold of the ship and do the job for which everything else had been only preliminaries.

Several days later the divers went back to the wreck, this time equipped with tools to widen the hole, trailing cables for hoisting the treasure aboard the salvage vessel.

A sight they tried not to believe greeted them. Of course the removal of the sand had created a hollow in the bottom . . . and the wreck had turned and slid into the hollow, with the gap in the hull at the bottom!

I don't know whether compressed air drills existed in 1913. They would have been the tool to use under the circumstances, all that had to be done was to make a sufficiently large hole in the undamaged side of the hull that was then topmost. Of course the National Salvage Association did not tell in fine detail just what they did—no use giving pointers to competitors. At any event they resumed work during the spring of 1914, without issuing any statements except the obvious one in August 1914 that operations would be suspended for the duration of the war.

To everybody's surprise, work was not resumed after the first World War, or if anything was done it must have been on such a minor scale that the newspapers did not say anything.

To the best of my knowledge the 20 million dollars in gold are still there—I shall refrain from paging Arthur C. Clarke at this point. One discovery of sunken treasure is enough per person. Besides, the gold of *La Lutine* does not need to be discovered. Even if currents of the sea should have shifted the position of the wreck it must be in an area corresponding to about a city block.

The two remaining questions are whether the recovery will still be worthwhile and how we would go about it nowadays.

The first question can be answered relatively easily. Gold

coins worth 20 million dollars in 1900 would be worth about 40 million dollars now—just considered as metal, that is. If the pieces were in new condition when they were loaded aboard the ship they would have a still higher value as collector's items, let's say about 110 million dollars.

As the finds of perfectly preserved Spanish doubloons in sunken ships just south of Cape Kennedy have proved once more, gold coins do not deteriorate in sea water.

In short, the salvage of the hoard of *La Lutine* would be worthwhile if the salvage operations can be carried out for less than 50 million dollars of current purchasing power. Whether that can be done would depend on the thickness of the sand layer on the wreck right now and the distance in feet from the surface of the North Sea at high tide to the wreck.

A modern salvage operation would probably try to keep the currents away from the wreck by building a wall around it. It would be quite similar to any dam-building operation, by dropping blocks of anything that is cheap and will not float. Once the wreck has been walled in there are two possibilities.

The more intriguing one would be to build up this wall to a few feet above high-tide level, making the wall waterproof with sheets of bitumen and concrete and pumping out the "well" so that salvage workers can go to work. But this would be the more expensive solution—and this also happens to be an area where storm-driven floods grow ten or twelve feet taller than normal high tide.

But one can work very nicely under water, if the water is quiet and not too deep. Of all the known sunken treasure ships the famous *La Lutine* rests at the shallowest depth. And a wall around the wreck would keep the water quiet. Maybe there are some people sitting around right now in Amsterdam or in London thinking about salvage.

Even if there aren't, it is still possible that the Dutch will salvage the treasure of *La Lutine* as a by-product of another

project. The string of islands along the Dutch coast, collectively known as the West Frisian Islands, indicates, as has
been said, the original coastline. The portion of the North Sea
between this string of islands and the mainland is known as
the *Waddenzee* and is quite shallow, though it is made difficult by fast-flowing currents. Ever since Dutch engineers succeeded in recovering the area covered for centuries by the
Zuider Zee, another set of Dutch engineers and scientists has
been dreaming about dams from Den Helder on the mainland to the island of Texel, then a dam from Texel to the
next island (Vlieland), then one between Vlieland and Terschelling, one from Terschelling to Ameland and finally one
from Ameland to the mainland.

At the moment this is not even a project, in spite of (or
possibly because of) cost estimates that have been made. But
eventually it will be done. And after it has been done *La
Lutine* will become accessible again. And her gold may help
to amortize the cost of the dam-building project a little bit
faster than cautious actuaries, who have to ignore such possibilities, have calculated.

3

The Great Pyramid,
The Golden Section and Pi

TO REASSURE ALL THOSE READERS who, when reading the above title, muttered to themselves that these three things have absolutely nothing to do with each other, I wish to state in this very first sentence that I agree with them. Of course neither the "golden section" nor *pi* is hidden in the structure which an ardent and effusive admirer once called the Miracle in Stone, using the word "miracle" in its literal religious meaning. But it is an interesting story how all the multitudinous misunderstandings surrounding the Great Pyramid originated.

That the pyramid of King Khufu was a major engineering and organizational accomplishment is something that does not need to be stressed.

It is not only astonishing that a structure of such size was built as early as it was; it is also astonishing how well it was built. As a matter of fact, Khufu's pyramid is of better workmanship than the later pyramids built on the same plateau, the so-called pyramid plateau of Giza, about six miles to the west of Cairo. Since Khufu was the first to build a pyramid in this particular locality, the whole plateau was originally named after him. It was called *Akhet Khufu*, or "Khufu's Horizon."

Why Khufu picked this particular locality for his pyramid is not known. That is, we don't know of any inscription saying that Pharaoh decreed this site because his fellow gods had told him to begin his soul-voyage after death from this place. But we can think of a number of eminently practical reasons why he chose this spot.

To begin with, he could see it from his summer palace and watch the actual work going on. Secondly, the location of the building site was such that, when the annual Nile flood occurred, the blocks of stone could be floated on rafts to the foot of the growing structure. Finally, most egyptologists (and especially the Egyptian egyptologists) believe that Khufu's pyramid hides an outcropping of natural rock which obviously saved that much work in the erection of a virtually solid structure.

Even so, 2,300,000 blocks of stone went into the pyramid, averaging 2½ tons in weight, with a few that must weigh about 15 tons each. The rock was quarried nearby. Professor Selim Hassan found some ancient quarries within easy walking distance of the pyramid.

Originally the pyramid had an outer casing of white limestone—Greek writers who saw it blinding white under the desert sun assumed that it was white limestone all the way through—which is now gone. Not completely gone, though; it merely is no longer a part of Khufu's pyramid, but forms portions of still-standing mosques.

Without its casing, the pyramid is 450 feet tall. We can't tell precisely how high it was originally.

The white limestone came from Turah, somewhat farther south and on the other side of the river, involving transportation over 14 miles of water. Some of the granite used in the interior came from Aswan, a good distance up-river, but again with the possibility of water transport.

It is the height of the structure which is responsible for its name. The Egyptians called this height *pyr-em-us*. The Greeks adapted the term to their tongue by pronouncing it *pyramis* and using it as a designation for that particular shape. Herodotus coined a plural, *pyramides*, from which, at a much later date, the current singular "pyramid" was derived.

Since we are on the subject of names, I am sorry to report that we don't really know how the name of the king was pronounced. The written form transliterates as *Hwfw* which, in order to be able to say it at all, is pronounced Khufu. Cheops (the "ch" should also be sounded as "kh") is the Greek form used by Herodotus.

Herodotus, incidentally, seems to have been the first who told stories about the pyramid which do not strictly jibe with the truth.

"One of the most frequently repeated stories," to quote Prof. Selim Hassan, from an article in the Egyptian monthly *The Scribe*, February, 1956, "is that in order to build the pyramid, Khufu closed the temples and enslaved the whole population to work as slave-laborers on its construction. This story has been going the rounds since the middle of the Fifth Century B.C., when the Greek traveler and historian Herodotus visited Egypt and evidently fell into the hands of a typical dragoman, who, like his modern descendants, thought that a few sensational stories would earn him a bigger tip from the gullible stranger."

They probably did, but because more than a score of centuries had gone by since the actual work, the Egyptian may easily have believed his own stories.

A dozen centuries after Herodotus, other travelers came and saw the pyramids. Apparently no stories were told any more, and though the travelers probably saw examples of hieroglyphic writing, there was nobody on Earth then who could read it. Consequently they wondered about the nature and the purpose of these structures.

Christian travelers, remembering their Bible, theorized that these must have been the giant storehouses for grain which Joseph had built to combat the forthcoming seven-year famine. Moslem philosophers remembered the older writings, too, but evolved a different explanation. There may have been kings not mentioned in these writings and the prophets of these kings must have told them about the future coming of the deluge. The kings then ordered the pyramids built as refuges from the coming flood.

Some less learned people reasoned that anything so massive must guard great wealth in gold and jewels, and they drew practical conclusions from their opinion, sometimes with success.

All these speculations dealt with pyramids in general, the pyramids of Egypt which extend over an area of 40 miles from north to south along the Nile (ten times as much if you include a few far to the south near Thebes and Edfu). The speculations of the last century are restricted to just one pyramid, that of Khufu.

The one who started it may have been, in all innocence, the famous astronomer Sir William Herschel. In his time, nobody knew just how old the pyramids were. The only thing that was certain was that they had already been old in the time of Herodotus. Herschel, learning that the entrance to the pyramid of Khufu formed a rather steep incline, may have been reminded of his telescopes and he wondered which star one might see if one were standing on the bottom of the entrance.

Some rather tedious calculations provided an answer. Looking through that shaft, an observer would have seen the star *alpha Draconis*, if the year were 2160 B.C. Herschel then stated that the pyramid may have been built in that year.

We now know that it is much older.

But Herschel's attempt to date the building of the pyramid on astronomical grounds took hold—long after his death.

It was in 1859 that John Taylor, a London publisher and book-dealer, published a book which he had written himself.

It bore the title *The Great Pyramid, Why was it built and Who built it?* His conclusion was that the pyramid had been built for the purpose of embodying a few important measurements. If Taylor had been an American, he might have said that it was the Egyptian equivalent of the Bureau of Standards, with the additional twist that all the standards are "classified information" not meant for the average dumb citizen.

In the course of his romancing, John Taylor discovered that the Egyptians must have used the same units of measurement as the English—or at least the more important of these units—and he succeeded in finding a unit which had been lost. In England at that time, a Quarter was used as a measurement for wheat. Taylor said, "A quarter of what?" and found the answer: The original "whole," four Quarters of wheat, was the "so-called" sarcophagus of the pharaoh.

Taylor also found that the height of the pyramid (which he overestimated by a few feet) was 1/270,000 of the circumference of the Earth. Here one can only say, "Why not?" for the height of the pyramid obviously must be some fraction of the circumference (or of the diameter) of the Earth.

Taylor was willing to admit that a few such things could be coincidences. To feel sure that it was planned, he looked for something which could not be a coincidence—or so he thought—and he found one, too. The square of the height of the pyramid, compared to the area of one of its triangular faces, demonstrated the "golden section."

That "golden section" had been around ever since the days of Euclid and had at irregular intervals taken hold of somebody's imagination. (At present, hardly anyone pays any attention to it.)

Let's first see what the term means (Fig. 7).

We have here a distance *AB* which is to be divided according to the golden section. To do so, we erect a vertical line in *B* which is precisely half as long as *AB*. The rest of

the construction can be read off the diagram. The result is
that the distance called the *minor* has the same proportion
to the *major* as the *major* has to the total, namely AB. And
if we now subtract the *minor* from the *major*, we have divided the *major* according to the golden section.

The golden section was publicized for the first time by an
Italian, Luca Pacioli, who may be the inventor of double-
entry bookkeeping; at any rate, this method appears in print
for the first time in one of his books. After having produced
this boon for tax collectors and merchants, he intended to
bestow a similar boon to artists with a book called *De Divina
Proportione*, published in 1509 with illustrations by his
friend Leonardo da Vinci.

Pacioli tried to show—and succeeded to a good extent—
that most of the things we consider "beautiful" are constructed in accordance with the golden section when broken
down into measurements. The numerical relationship of the
golden section is 5 to 8 and, for centuries, all books did cor-
respond to it. European books still do, at least more often
than American books. The only book in my library which is
of American origin and which shows that proportion is the
World Almanac.

The next time the golden section was consciously "redis-
covered" by the artists, or more precisely by the theorists of
art, was around the middle of the nineteenth century, just
the time in which John Taylor wrote. It cannot be said that
his book was a success and it probably would have been forgotten completely if it had not been for Charles Piazzi
Smyth, at that time Astronomer Royal for Scotland.

Smyth was the son of an admiral and he happened to be
born in Italy. His godfather at the christening was Father
Giuseppe Piazzi, the discoverer of the asteroid Ceres, the first
asteroid to be found. Father Piazzi said then that he hoped
that the child would become an astronomer.

Charles Piazzi Smyth did become an astronomer and, as an astronomer, he made important contributions to spectroscopy, then a very new science. He also deserves much credit for advocating an innovation which now seems obvious to us —building observatories on high mountains.

At the age of forty, Smyth came across John Taylor's book and became enchanted with it. Thinking and dreaming about it, he quickly convinced himself that Taylor had barely scratched the surface. He thought and calculated and worked and, in 1864, he wrote a 600-page book called *Our Inheritance in the Great Pyramid.*

It was a great success and its awed readers learned that the main item in the plan for the Great Pyramid had been nothing less than the squaring of the circle. Smyth said that the bottom square of the pyramid represented—or, rather, was equal to—the circumference of a circle drawn with the height of the pyramid as its radius.

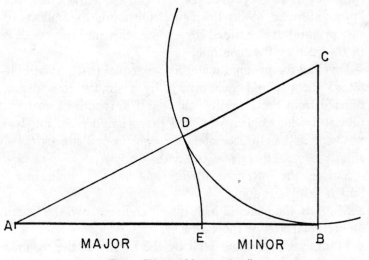

Fig. 7. The "golden section."

Whoever read this with a critical or just an open eye should have stopped right there. Maybe the base of the pyramid measured 3055.24 feet, as Prof. Smyth said, but how about the height? The outer casing and with it the point of the pyramid were missing. Therefore the height could not be measured directly. Of course if the casing had been there, one could have measured the slope angle and calculated the height from that.

The slope angle must have been near 52°, so Smyth said that it originally was 51° 51′ 14.3″ which produced a height of 486.256 feet. Therefore the ratio of height to circumference corresponded to two *pi*. Insisting that this could not be a coincidence and apparently unaware of the fact that he himself had not *found* the figure but *put it in*, Smyth went on to other discoveries.

At the base, one side of the pyramid measured 763.81 feet. The Egyptians naturally had not used feet as a unit of measurement; it must have been something else. Smyth divided these 763.81 feet by 365.2422 and got a unit he called the "pyramid meter." Why this figure? Obviously the builders of the pyramid had wanted to express the number of days in the year by the base line.

Dividing the pyramid meter into 25 equal parts, Smyth obtained the pyramid inch, which, by a strange coincidence, differed from the English inch by just 1/1000th of an inch. Obviously the English still used the pyramid inch, but had not kept its length accurately through the millennia. It had shrunk by 1/10th of one per cent.

Having the "pyramid meter" and the "pyramid inch," Smyth really got going.

Multiply the pyramid inch by 10^7 and you have the length of the polar axis of the Earth.

Multiply the pyramid inch by the height of the pyramid (in pyramid inches, of course) and then multiply that figure by 10⁹ and you get the distance from the Earth to the Sun. (The result is 91.84 million miles, which is neither perihelion nor aphelion nor mean distance.)

Express the cubic content of the pyramid in cubic inches and you have the total number of all people that have lived on Earth since the Creation.

As for the so-called sarcophagus, it was not only the original standard for volumetric measurements, according to Smyth. It was more. Its volume, expressed in cubic pyramid meters, was precisely 5.7, which looks like a wrong figure until you realize that this is the specific gravity of the Earth as a whole! (Actually the density of the Earth is 5.52.)

One reader, by profession an engineer, wrote later that Smyth's treatise cost him the better part of a night and that it had the result that he "did not fall asleep in my bed but in a medley of endless decimals, triangles and circles, complicated by polar diameters and astronomical distances; dealing with empty granite sarcophagi and pharaohs with mile-long measuring rods marching through space with the luminous eyes of prophets."

He realized that Smyth had "found" his "cosmic figures" in the pyramid by putting them in in the first place. But he also said that he had the faint feeling that something still needed to be explained.

It was explained several decades later by the egyptologist Ludwig Borchardt, who approached the whole problem from the opposite direction. He asked just what unit the Egyptians had actually used in building. Moreover, he wanted to know just how far advanced their mathematics had been.

As for the unit of measurement, he found that they used the ell. There was a minor complication in that it seemed that they had used two different kinds of ells. One had a length of seven palms, the other of six palms. Although the six-palm ell corresponds better to reality (an ell is the length from the elbow to the tip of the longest finger), the seven-palm ell was used for construction, at least for large buildings.

In our measurement, the "royal ell" of seven palms is a little less than 21 inches. Borchardt used 525 millimeters as an approximation. Then the palm would be 75 millimeters or just about three inches. Each palm, in turn, was divided into four fingers, which would measure 19 millimeters each if the figure for the royal ell of 525 millimeters is accepted. At any event, the ell had seven palms or 28 "fingers."

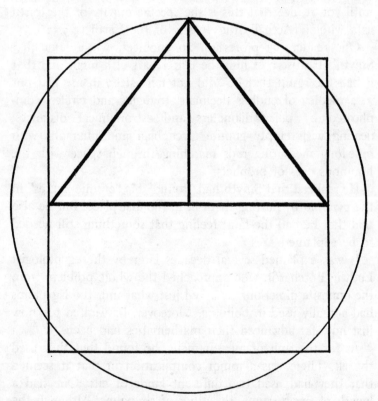

Fig. 8. *Piazzi Smyth's construction of squaring the circle with the aid of the Great Pyramid.*

As regards Egyptian arithmetic, we know that they could handle simple fractions like ½, ⅓, ¼, etc., and fractions like ¾ (namely 1 minus ¼) or ⅔ (1 minus ⅓). When it comes to pyramids, we have a few examples in the famous *Papyrus Rhind* which, while old, is probably a good deal younger than the pyramid.

Example No. 56 in the *Papyrus Rhind* requested the pupil to calculate the slope of a pyramid with a base length of 360 ells and a height of 250 ells. A modern high school boy would reach for the logarithm table and come up (unless he made a mistake) with the answer 54° 14′ 46″. The Egyptian advanced pupil answered 5 1/25 palms.

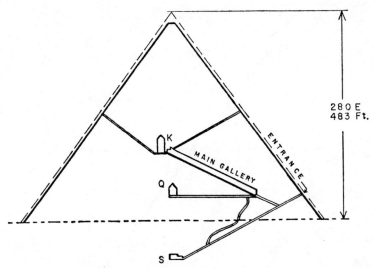

280 E
483 Ft.

Fig. 9. Cross section of Khufu's pyramid. S means an abandoned burial chamber (unfinished), Q is the so-called Queen's chamber, never used, K the King's chamber. The two shafts to the King's chamber were for ventilation.

Example No. 58 said that the base length was 140 ells and the height 93⅓ ells. The answer was 5¼ palms.

And example No. 59 (no doubt dealing with a backyard pyramid) gave 12 ells as the length of the base line and 8 ells as the height. The answer was also 5¼ palms.

What do these answers mean?

The answer is given in Fig. 10. The answer meant that the slope of the pyramid was so many palms from a vertical line one ell in height. That this is correct is proved by the fact that measuring triangles for the use of builders and masons have been found which corresponded to slopes of 5, 5¼, etc., palms, all rather awkward angles if expressed in degrees and minutes of arc.

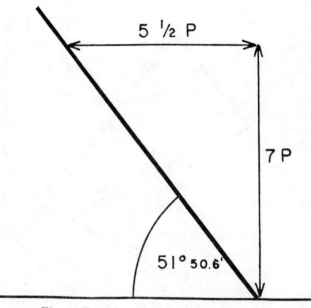

Fig. 10. Egyptian method of measuring angles.

The slope of the Great Pyramid was quite close to 52°. For lack of the casing, one could not be any more precise than that. A slope of 5½ palms produces an angle of 51° 50.6′.

And that would have made the pyramid 280 ells high, a neat, even figure—in Egyptian measurements, that is.

Now remember that John Taylor had proclaimed that the pyramid represented the golden section. Prof. Smyth had proclaimed that it represented *pi*. Since it cannot possibly do both, Borchardt calculated what the respective angles would have to be and how the measurements would have come out in Egyptian ells. The result surprised everybody. You find it clearly demonstrated in this table:

SLOPE

	for *pi*	for 5½ palms	golden section
slope angle	51° 51.2′	51° 50.6′	51° 49.6′
slope (Egyptian)	4.4979 P.	5.5000 P.	5.5032 P.
base line for 280 ells height	439.82 E.	440 E.	440.24 E.

Small wonder that people were led astray if the *pi* slope, the golden section slope and the simple Egyptian slope were practically the same. They are so much alike that it is impossible to distinguish them on a drawing of anything like publishable size.

That they did not "intend" to build a *pi* slope is also clear from the *Papyrus Rhind*, where the ratio we now call *pi* appears in examples No. 41, 48 and 50 in the form that 8/9th of the diameter of a circle is the side of a square of equal area. In our notation, this makes *pi* equal to 3.1604, which is too large. If they had tried for the *pi* slope, it would have been a different pyramid, considering their idea of the value of *pi*. There is no way of saying whether they knew the golden section, but it is not even remotely likely.

We are left then with the realization that Khufu's builders were extremely skilled workers, but that they did not try to hide any cosmic secrets. And where did they acquire their skill? Well, while the Great Pyramid is the biggest and one of the oldest pyramids, there had been considerable practice in building before. The pyramid had forerunners, called mastabas (Fig. 11).

No. 1 shows a cross section of the mastaba of King Mena of the First Dynasty. It is just a subterranean burial chamber covered by a solid slab of mud brick. No. 2 is the mastaba of King Djer of the First Dynasty and No. 3 the mastaba of King Den, also of the First Dynasty. You can see how the pyramid shape was gradually approached. No. 4 is the tomb of King Zoser of the Third Dynasty; I called it "tomb" for, as can

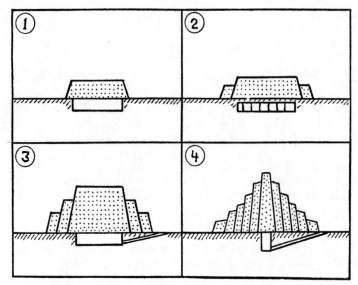

Fig. 11. *Forerunner of the pyramids, the mastabas.*

be seen, it is hard to decide whether this was still a rather complicated mastaba or a pyramid without casing.

The first pyramid which did have a casing, filling in the steps, was that of King Snefru of the Fourth Dynasty, the same dynasty to which King Khufu belonged.

I said earlier that Herodotus was probably told a tall tale

when he was informed that the whole nation was drafted by Khufu to build his pyramid. It was an unlikely story in the first place, for one can assume that a pharaoh knew better than to ruin all commerce for years.

But then who did provide the muscle power? No doubt that slaves did work on the pyramid; this is only logical for a slaveholding society. But slaves in general also had other vital things to do.

The most likely answer is that the local *fellahin*, the peasants, were employed once a year.

When the Nile flooded the country, the circumstances were proper for floating in the building blocks. And it was also the time when the *fellahin* had to sit idle, precisely because their fields were flooded, making it logical to employ them for this period. Maybe the word "employ" is not quite right. They were probably drafted. But we now know that they were paid, mostly in food and clothing.

It is still probable that the overseers carried whips. But they also carried, in the last stages of the building, the triangles made for a slope of 5½ palms per ell of vertical height, the proportion which was destined to cause so much confusion thousands of years later.

4

Who Invented the Crossbow?

IT IS SIMPLY IMPOSSIBLE to find an article on crossbows or medieval warfare that neglects to mention that the Second Lateran Council, in 1139, forbade the use of the crossbow to Christians—except for hunting or against infidels—and that Pope Innocentius III, later in the same century, reaffirmed this *prohibitus est*. British writers, as a rule, add the information that the crossbow was introduced in England in 1066 by the invading Normans, but that it never became as popular in England as it was on the continent.

While saying all this, most writers create the impression—and seem to be under that impression themselves—that the crossbow must have been a fairly recent invention at the time the Lateran Council adjourned. Since it is certain that crossbows existed at a much earlier time, it is logical to assume that the weapon achieved a sudden surge in popularity around the year 1100, leading to ecclesiastical measures. Such sudden surges are usually the result of an improvement of some kind, and the most likely improvement for that period was the introduction of a steel bow instead of a wooden bow.

If the older crossbows had wooden bows, they either had to be so large as to be unwieldy or, if small enough, both their range and their penetrating power must have been inferior to the normal bow. As a matter of fact British writers have occasionally wondered in print why the crossbow became popular at all. Even at the height of its development a crossbow bolt did not carry much farther than an arrow from a longbow, and both could penetrate a shield that a man could carry. Moreover, a good longbow man could get off ten arrows in the time a crossbow man could shoot three bolts. All true; but a man who had never used a crossbow would be a good shot after three weeks of five hours of training every day, while an archery apprentice with a longbow was still a beginner after the same amount of practice.

So there was a good reason for the popularity of the crossbow, after the introduction of steel had made it at least equal in power to a heavy longbow in the hands of a strong man.

It is true that references to crossbows prior to the famous edict of the Lateran Council are rare, but they exist. Roman writers had occasionally mentioned a weapon they called *manuballista* or *arcuballista* . . . but there could be some doubt whether the term actually referred to crossbows. Considered as a word, *"manuballista"* just meant a device that threw something and that a warrior held in (or operated with) his hands, and that still left many possibilities open. But such doubts were resolved in 1831. During that year a Roman burial monument with bas reliefs was found near Polignac sur Loire in France; it was later brought to the museum at Puy, and artists could sketch the bas reliefs. Among them was an unmistakable crossbow, complete with *pharetra*, the Roman term for a quiver, as shown in Fig. 12. Unfortunately the artist who made the bas relief must have been poorly acquainted with the weapon, for most of the things one would dearly like to know are simply not shown. It is not clear, for example, whether this crossbow was bent by hand or whether a mechanical device of some kind was needed. And the most interesting part, the lock mechanism, is hardly indicated.

Nor can the age of the monument be established. Its location in France indicates that the burial took place while the Romans extended over all of western Europe, but this leaves a leeway of several centuries.

Fortunately we are on much firmer ground with another

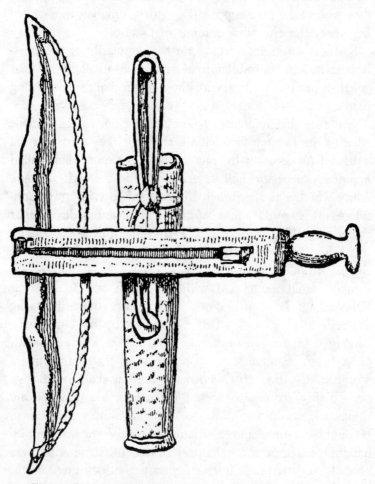

Fig. 12. Picture of a crossbow from a Roman grave in France.

ancient crossbow (Fig. 13.) that goes under the Greek name of *gastrophetes*; it is a bit disappointing that this impressive-sounding word just means "belly gun." But at least there is

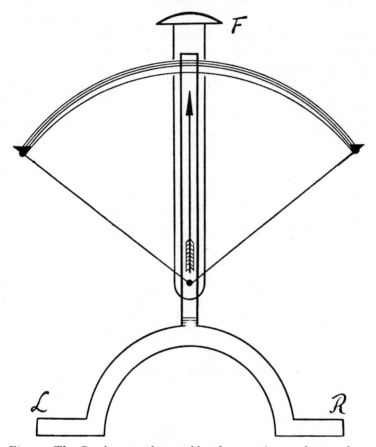

Fig. 13. The Greek gastrophetes, oldest known picture of a crossbow.

a reason for this name. The "belly gun" was cocked by resting the front end (F) of the slide on the ground and leaning the body weight on the semicircle between the two pieces

L and R, which may have been resting on the shoulders of the man while shooting the weapon.

We know about the *gastrophetes* from what is left of the writings of one Ktesibios. Though there were several people by that name, it is pretty certain that the Ktesibios in question is the one who lived during the reign of Ptolemy Physkon (170-117 B.C.), which makes him a contemporary of Philon of Byzantium, another writer who has supplied us with some information about the weapons then in use. Philon's *Belopoiika*—also known as his Fourth Book on Mechanics—did not say anything about crossbows, at least not in the portions of his work that we still have. But he wrote at length about catapults. The Greek experts who had the Prussian Academy of Sciences reissue the work (Greek original with German translation) in 1918 pointed out that Philon's style was clumsy and redundant and that he often sounds pleased that he managed to explain something. Personally I wonder whether Philon's clumsy and redundant style was the result of trying hard to explain difficult concepts to practical men who were handy with tools but not literary lights.

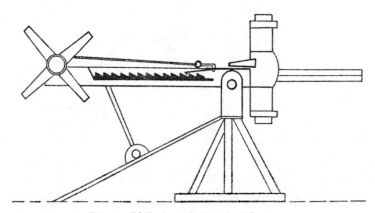

Fig. 14. Philon's euthytonon, *side view.*

At any event Philon carefully described two of the weapons of his time, the *euthytonon* and the *palintonon*. They were fairly much alike, except that the *euthytonon* (see Figs. 14 and 15) shot large arrows while the *palintonon* threw round stones. Very likely the *euthytonon* was used for pointblank shooting when the enemy actually attacked, while the *palintonon* was used to harass the enemy while he was behind fortified positions.

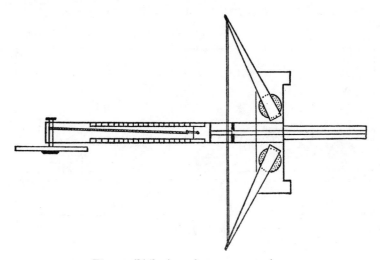

Fig. 15. Philon's euthytonon, *top view.*

The construction of the *euthytonon* was quite advanced, and Philon's description makes one thing quite clear: it was *not* a large crossbow. In the crossbow, from the *gastrophetes* to the modern target crossbow, the energy is stored into bending something flexible, wood or steel. In the *euthytonon*, and in all similar weapons that were built for the next sixteen centuries to come, the arms are not flexible but rigid. The energy is stored in skeins of cord, or strips of rawhide or horsehair that are twisted around the end of these rigid

arms. The bow is not bent—in fact, there is no bow to begin with—but elastic skeins are twisted. As the pictures show,
the weapon was wound up by means of a small windlass. Two
ratchet hooks saw to it that the weapon did not become un-
wound just because a hand slipped on the spokes of the windlass. The final catch (Fig. 16) consists of a hook that admits
the string of the catapult but could not hold it under tension.
It is made secure by sliding a piece of metal (black in Fig.
16) under it. To discharge the weapon this piece of metal
was yanked out or knocked out by a hammer blow.

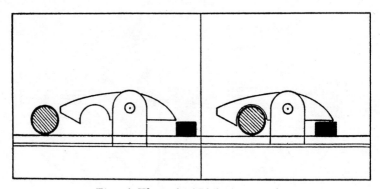

Fig. 16. The lock of Philon's catapult.

A mechanism involving a sudden jerk or blow was, of
course, impossible with a portable weapon since it would
spoil the aim. The crossbow makers of the Middle Ages came
up with a different mechanism that is usually referred to as
the "revolving nut" (Fig. 17). While the crossbow is being
bent, or wound up, or cocked, the revolving nut has the position shown at left. The string of the bow, still being tensed,
slowly turns it until it has reached the position shown at
right, at which point a steel piece at the bottom goes into
action and locks it. This strip of steel is connected with the

trigger. The trigger of a crossbow used to be large, and in most models the trigger was not slowly pulled back as in modern firearms, but lifted in the direction of the stock of the crossbow.

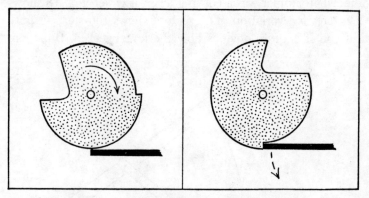

Fig. 17. The "revolving nut" of the medieval crossbow.

Now, the whole point of the crossbow was that it was powerful. Its string could not simply be pulled back by the action of four fingers as in an ordinary bow. To bend a crossbow needed at the very least both hands of the sharpshooter; this led to the strange distinction of a "one foot crossbow" and a "two feet crossbow." The one foot crossbow had a stirrup attached to its front end. The crossbow man placed this stirrup on the ground, put one foot into it and pulled the string up with both hands until it caught in the revolving nut. For the more powerful "two feet crossbow" both feet were needed to steady the weapon. For this reason the bow was attached right to the front end of the stock so that the crossbow man could place one foot on each side of the stock when bending the bow.

For the still more powerful versions even this was not enough. They were equipped with a small windlass or a so-called cranequin, a wind-up device that was placed on top of the crossbow prior to cocking it. Of course it had to be removed prior to shooting, which did not increase the frequency with which bolts could be thrown against the enemy. Somewhat simpler was a cocking lever of which Fig. 18 shows an interesting variation. The picture shows the starting position and it is quite obvious how the lever worked. But then,

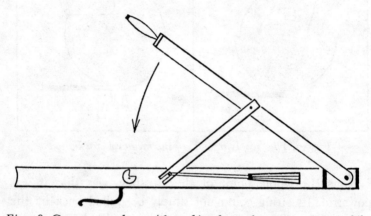

Fig. 18. *German crossbow with cocking lever that gave support while shooting.*

once the crossbow was cocked, the lever (which could also be detached completely) was folded down over the front end to provide a support. With a 30-inch lever the support was too short for shooting while standing, but it had just the right length for shooting from a kneeling position.

Since crossbows of the more powerful types had ranges up to 350 yards, especially when shot by the defenders of a castle or a walled city who had the advantage of an elevation of thirty feet or more over the attackers, the siege engines that were the descendants of the *euthytonon* and *palintonon* had to have a slightly longer range, say 400 yards or better.

Siege engines, ballistas and catapults, blidas and springardes, mangonals and trebuchets—they have a multitude of names, and in most cases we can be sure what a manuscript really means only if we have a sketch to go along with the description. There are at least two reasons for the multitude of names: Italian words that may have had Latin or Greek roots originally were adapted by the French to their own tongues, then the Germans took either the Italian or the French form, and sometimes both, and Germanized them. Then, twenty or fifty years later somebody would translate the term into German, not always skillfully. In addition to this problem of overlapping languages, pride played a role. Some small army, say, had two large siege engines of which they were, naturally, quite proud. So they were given names, like ships. But if these names were in any way unusual, a chronicler half a century later and living elsewhere, might think that these were special types of siege engines. Mistaken translations and misunderstood names lengthened the lists.

The same thing happened, a few centuries later, with real guns, until finally the gunnery master of the city of Frankfurt am Main, Leonhart Fronsperger by name, cried out in despair: "Of all the guns that are pulled into the field there are just eight [types], four wall breakers and four field pieces, and even if you give a thousand names to them there are still just eight and not more." Master Gunner Fronsperger classified his guns by the weight of shot; we'll have to classify the siege engines by types to get anywhere.

The confusion must have started early because an otherwise very competent book states that there were only two types originally: one which the Romans called *catapultus* and the Greeks *Katapeltes* and another one which the Romans called *ballista* and the Greeks *lithobolos*.

Now, *lithobolos* is easy to translate; it means "stone thrower"—that would be the *palintonon* of Philon. As for the word *katapeltes* an attempt at translation is a little more difficult. There was a very similar Greek military term that meant "to overrun" (an enemy position); but the name may also be derived from the two Greek words for "down" and for "shield." In either case one is reminded of Philon's *euthytonon*. But from the engineering point of view the arrow-shooting and the stone-throwing devices were one and the same thing. Both *looked* like crossbows; both had rigid arms and were wound by means of a windlass. And in both the energy was stored by twisting skeins of a flexible material.

Since it was torsion that did the work, the whole family of siege engines—"and even if they bore a thousand names" —should be referred to as the "torsion engines." A one-armed torsion engine, the ones called "catapults" in historical novels and movies, is shown as Fig. 19. Here a very large

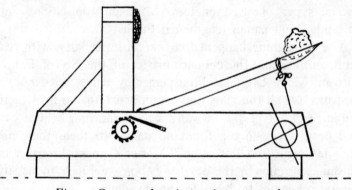

Fig. 19. One-armed torsion engine or catapult.

"spoon" had its handle inserted in a horizontal skein of raw-hide strips and, when released, struck a horizontal and padded member. The main advantage of this type of weapon was that almost anything could be put into the hollow of the spoon: rocks, inflammable substances, trussed-up dead animals and anything else that might be handy.

In all of these siege engines all the tension just prior to shooting was sustained by a single rope. In the movies a burly but somehow noble looking warrior stands by with a sharp sword or a hefty battle axe to sever this rope. In reality the armorers of the Middle Ages used the slip-hook (Fig. 20)

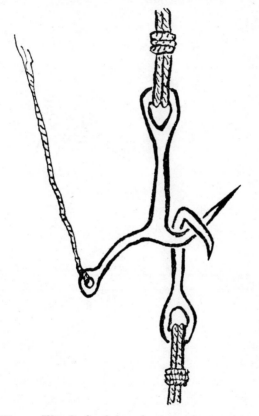

Fig. 20. The slip-hook for releasing a siege engine.

that parted reliably when yanked sideways and that could be reused any number of times.

And now we come to the second type of siege engine,

called trebuchet by the French and blida (pronounced like
"bleeder") by the Germans. Technically this was a counterweight engine (Fig. 21). A sturdy wooden basket with a
heavy metal frame was filled with rocks, then the long throwing arm was pulled down by means of a winch, and the mis-
sile was placed on a spoon or basket at the end.

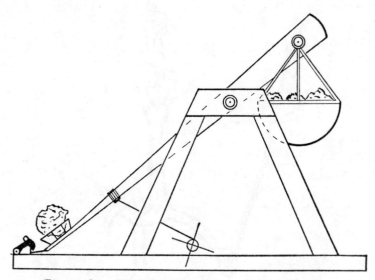

Fig. 21. Counterweight engine, also known as Trebuchet.

Many medieval pictures show a sling attached to the end
of the throwing arm, and it is stated that this sling extended
the length of the arm and therefore the range. But since such
a sling had to open at just the right moment I have severe
doubts that it was used often. In a small model which I
helped to build when I was in high school the sling simply
never opened. For this reason I look at pictures of trebuchets
with slings as "artist's conceptions" that picture an idea
rather than reality.

The final type of siege engine, Fig. 22, went under names like espringale, espringold or springarde. Here the energy was

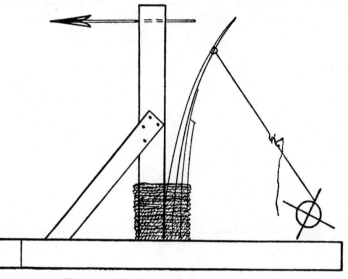

Fig. 22. A "Springarde," or spear thrower.

stored by bending a piece of wood which, when released, would strike a heavy spear and propel it over a range comparable to that of other such devices. It probably could not be aimed well, but it had the advantage that it was easy to build on the spot. The armorer only had to carry a rope, a winch with ratchet and a slip-hook, and the spears, of course. But this was the only type of siege engine which resembled the bow and the crossbow in function by storing the energy in bending wood. The torsion engines, though they resembled crossbows in appearance were something different. But the crossbow probably took its shape from them; the first crossbows indubitably were just extra heavy bows mounted on a stock.

The *gastrophetes* of Ktesibios is the earliest example of which we have documentary evidence. But the crossbow did not become important until more than a thousand years later when somebody, flexing a fine sword, thought of substituting a steel bow for the wooden one.

5

Dead or Alive?

DURING THE EARLY PART of the eighteenth century some very vague rumors about gigantic bones reached Paris. Unaccompanied by any evidence, these rumors traveled via Spain, for they originated from Argentina. Shorn of embroidery and conjecture, they stated that large bones could be found in the pampas. These were said to be as large as the bones of elephants.

The gentlemen of the Academy in Paris decided that it was best not to say anything. As far as anybody knew, there were no elephants in the Americas. Still, South America was not well explored yet, so—let the Spaniards prove their case if they have one.

It so happened that they did.

During the earlier years of the 18th century only occasional single bones had been seen by literate men, usually in places where a river cut into the soil of the pampas. In 1789 a complete skeleton was found, fortunately not too far from Buenos Aires, at a place called Lujan. The viceroy ordered that the bones be excavated and sent to Madrid. There a scientist named Garriga assembled them and, in 1796, published a first description.

The animal had been about the size of an elephant, or would have been if its legs had been a little longer. It stood eight feet tall at the shoulder and had an overall length of 14 feet.

The first thing that impressed Garriga was the legs, but not because they were beautiful. The bones were incredibly heavy, far more massive than the corresponding bones of an elephant. The tail was also very massive and long for a big animal (which usually have tiny tails) because it was long enough to just touch the ground. But while the comparison with an elephant was obvious because of the size, it broke down when it came to the foot skeleton and the skull. They did not resemble anything ever seen before, at least not in such a size. The skull showed clearly that this giant was a sloth.

Now it needed a name, which was compounded from the two Greek words for "large" (*megas*) and "mammal" (*therion*) in the Latinized version of *Megatherium americanum*.

Naturally things did not stop with this first skeleton. Pictures of it got into books, partly because it was the first and partly because it was so big.

More discoveries were made and scientists soon knew that there had been several species of giant sloth. The second species to be definitely established was *Mylodon robustus*, which was 11 feet long and differed from Megatherium mostly in having forelegs about as long as its hindlegs; in Megatherium the forelegs are a good deal longer than the hindlegs.

The third species was named *Mylodon gracilis*. Now the word *gracilis* would normally be translated as "dainty," but in this case the normal, or any other, translation just did not apply. The animal was by no means "dainty." It was a heavy-boned nine-foot monster.

It is possible that *gracilis* was used merely as the opposite of *robustus*. It is more likely that this name is a case of Teutonic humor, for the man who coined it was Professor Hermann Burmeister, of Germany, who had gone to South America on a trip of exploration and then decided to stay and settle down, mostly because of Megatherium and Mylodon.

Hermann Burmeister was fifty years old when he made this decision (in 1861 or 1862), but he still managed to enjoy thirty-one years of residence in the country he adopted for zoological reasons. When I state that he "enjoyed" these years, I do not use the term loosely. According to all accounts, life in Prof. Burmeister's house was friendly, witty and gay, and it was permanently open to any fellow scientist and any intelligent layman who was willing to talk Megatherium and other pampas fossils. That there could possibly ever be a shortage of domestic or imported wines never occurred to Burmeister, unless he had nightmares, which seems unlikely.

Burmeister's closest scientific associate and his successor (when Burmeister died in 1892 at the age of 85) was Professor Florentino Ameghino. Up to 1892, expert descriptions of pampas fossils had been in German; from then on, they were in Spanish. But behind all the scientific gaiety and the fun and thrill of a steady stream of discoveries there was one unanswered question. How old were the bones Burmeister and Ameghino dug up, cleaned, measured, assembled and described?

This question at that time was simply unanswerable, but Burmeister thought that while he could not name a figure, he could at least give an answer of sorts.

There was general agreement that man had originated in Asia and invaded the American double continent via the Bering Strait. This naturally meant that man had arrived in South America much later than in North America, since he had to traverse the length of the North American continent first. Any figures which were then mentioned were naturally guesses; man had probably arrived at the northern end of South America 3000 to 5000 years ago. Burmeister based his answer on this figure.

Man and Megatherium had never met, Burmeister was convinced, because the natives did not have any recollection of such animals and had invented a legend to account for the bones. They thought that the large animal was something like a gigantic mole which was instantly killed by sunlight if it inadvertently "broke surface."

Burmeister's ideas might have been well reasoned, but the facts were against him. Megatherium, the giant sloth, was very often associated with a giant armadillo—Glyptodon— and the two animals had obviously lived at the same time. But remains of Glyptodon and human artifacts were sometimes found together, and the prize discovery was a human skeleton sitting inside the giant carapace of a Glyptodon. This was certainly an ancient form of burial for somebody of importance. Finally, a skeleton of Megatherium was unearthed which was incomplete in a significant manner. The four legs were there and undisturbed, but most of the other bones were missing, and there had been a fire in the center, between the legs. It was perfectly apparent that here was a giant sloth that had been caught in a pit and roasted right in the trap from above.

There was no doubt then that the early South American Indians had known Megatherium "in the flesh," but it still did not answer the question: when had this happened?

In the meanwhile something else had taken place which did not seem to have a connection for a long time. By coincidence, another German who had made his home in South America figures in this section of the story, though not as prominently by far as Professor Burmeister.

Near the southern end of Patagonia there is a fjord or inlet —locally called a "canal"—with the gloomy name of Ultima Esperanza (Last Hope). There the retired German sea captain Eberhard bought himself some land and built a house. Visitors to the Eberhard ranch noticed that the hide of a large animal was hanging over some bushes. Some of these visitors—or so it was told later—tried to cut a piece off that hide, which proved to be extraordinarily difficult. The reason was that a large number of bean-sized "bones" were embedded in the hide. If any one of these visitors had been a naturalist, this fact would have done more than just make him suspicious; but evidently nobody, including Captain Eberhard, had any profound knowledge of natural history.

At some time—the date is uncertain, but it was after Burmeister's death—such a piece of skin reached Ameghino. It has never been established whether this particular piece came from the Eberhard ranch; Ameghino himself did not think so. The important thing was that this piece of skin was, or looked, fresh. Not fresh like animal skin in a butcher shop, but rather like untanned hide in a saddler's establishment. In any case it certainly was not fossil and Ameghino decided that logic, however incredible, had to prevail. A piece of Mylodon skin proved that the animal still existed somewhere.

Ameghino called a press conference. Newspapers around the world carried articles which declared: "The Giant Sloth Is not Extinct." The very fact that this animal, which for so many years had been so proverbially extinct, was supposed to be still alive set thought going in various directions at once.

Was there any evidence in addition to the piece of skin?

Did somebody in the past mention the giant sloth in any manner, probably with a native name which conveyed no meaning to readers elsewhere?

And, finally, where can they be found, to be captured for a zoological garden?

Professor Ameghino said that he did have additional evidence. Besides his piece of skin from an unknown source, there was the Ultima Esperanza hide. And then there was the story told by Ramón Lista, onetime Governor of Santa Cruz—he was later killed by Indians.

Lista reported that he had been with a hunting party in the interior of Patagonia. While camping at night, he and his party had seen an unknown animal which looked somewhat like a pangolin, except that it was covered with long hair.

The animal escaped, even though the hunters shot at it with their rifles.

Since Ramón Lista was a learned man with much experience in Patagonia (he wrote several books about his land which received high praise and are said to be still worthwhile reading), a story like this deserved attention. Strangely enough, Ameghino at first disregarded it, thinking that Lista must have been somehow mistaken. But then he suddenly changed his mind. A while later he even coined the scientific name *Neomylodon listai* (Lista's New Mylodon) and pointed out that it was quite possible that one or more of the hunters' shots had hit, but that they did no harm because of the bony nodules in a Mylodon's hide.

Then a native legend about a *Iemish* was dragged into the giant sloth debate and things really became confused. The *Iemish* was claimed to be a large beast that lived both on land and in the water, usually hiding in the water. It was a flesh-eater and drowned horses to eat them. Or else the *Iemish* was a beast the size of an ox that was harmless and nocturnal. During the day it slept in burrows which it had dug with its large claws. Finally somebody supplied Ameghino with a "translation" of the word *Iemish:* it was supposed to mean "the one with little stones on it." Ameghino thought that all this went together beautifully and could apply only to the *Neomylodon listai* that he had named.

All this, however, did not go together beautifully. An animal is either a flesh-eater, in which case it can't be called harmless, or it is harmless, in which case it is not likely to be a flesh-eater. But while this could be reasoned out by logic alone, it took an enormous amount of work to establish how the confusion had taken place.

The legend of the *Iemish,* the one that often retreats into the water and is a flesh-eater, refers essentially to the jaguar, which is a carnivore and does swim well. It probably also contains some confusion with the giant river otter of South America, which is of nearly the same size, is also carnivorous, like all otters, and, like all otters, lives in the water. The names which could be found in dictionaries that sound like *iemish* mostly are native words for "otter."

Of course the word does not translate the way Ameghino reported. It seems to be simply a name. But Ameghino, having been handed this significant-looking "translation" by somebody, made the mistake of applying the name *iemish* to the other legend about the ox-sized harmless nocturnal animal. (It might be added that the two legends did not exist in the same place. Their origins were 1500 or more miles apart.)

Ameghino, after having made this mistake, concluded that he had taken care of the question of available evidence. Then he set out to answer the second question; namely, whether the giant sloth might not have been mentioned by early writers on South America under another and probably native name. Here he was not only far more careful, he was also more successful.

He came across a book entitled *Historia de la Conquista del Paraguay, Rio de la Plata y Tucumàn* by Father Pedro Lozano, S.J., published 1740-1746, in which an animal *su* or *succarath* was mentioned. It was said to be large and to have the habit of carrying its young on its back. The natives were stated to hunt it in spite of the dangers involved, for they wanted its skin to make durable cloaks.

Hardly anybody in Europe had ever heard of Father Lozano before, but when Ameghino reported on the *su* in professional journals, all European zoologists had an automatic reaction. They knew the *su*. Its picture, however fantastic, was on the title page of the enormous zoology book by the Swiss savant Konrad Gesner which every one of the Europeans had read.

There in volume one of Gesner's *Historia animalium* (published in Zürich in 1955) one could find a paragraph headed *De Subo* ("Of the Su") which translates as follows:

> The Most Obnoxious Animal that might be seen, called Su in the New Lands. There is a place in the newly found land where lives a people calling itself in its language Patagones, and since the land is not very warm they cover themselves with fur from an animal they call Su, which means Water, by reason of its dwelling mainly near water. It is very dreadful, obnoxious, as may be seen. When hunted by the hunters, it take its young upon its back, covers them with its long tail and thus flees. It is caught in pits and killed with arrows.

This had made no sense until the fight about the still-living giant sloth started; now things had changed so that Gesner's paragraph *might* make an exciting kind of sense.

As long as nobody had paid much attention to Gesner's paragraph as a whole, even less attention had been paid to a note which said that this description had been taken from "Andreas Theuetus." Since Gesner wrote in Latin, it was only logical that he used the Latinized form; actually this was the name of André Thévet. Thévet's paragraph on the Su is the same as Gesner's naturally, but Thévet has one more sentence telling what happens after a su has fallen into a pit:

> When it sees that it is caught, it maims and kills its young (as if maddened) and gives such terrible cries that it makes the Savages very fearful and timid. Yet in the end they kill it with arrows and then they flay it.

Incidentally, each of the learned men made a linguistic mistake. Gesner did not know that the name of the Patagonians is not derived from their own language, and Thévet was wrong in thinking that *su* means water. Its meaning is "covering." Ameghino came close by translating *su* as "cloak." Thévet is the only literary source which might be construed as referring to a giant sloth. If one wants to accept it—and

I don't see why not—one of the smaller forms of giant sloth must have been still alive in the southern part of South America during the Middle Ages.

There are two more things: Where did the hide on Captain Eberhard's ranch come from?

Well, Captain Eberhard himself located a cave some distance from his home. The cave was almost completely closed (one could just squeeze through) by a wall of boulders which was obviously piled up by people. Inside the cave, the amateur explorers found a human skeleton, two more hides, and what is generally called a kitchen midden. Later, professional investigators discovered Mylodon droppings over a foot deep, and when they went to work on these droppings, they saw that they contained ends of plant stalks which had been *cut*. The teeth of the animals could not have produced such a clean end.

One of the investigators, Professor Santiago Roth, then proposed to rename the animal *Grypotherium domesticum*, since the Indians had apparently domesticated it. This would not have been impossible by itself, but there is one major fact that speaks against the idea: domesticated animals do not become extinct! Man sees to it that they don't. If the Indians had widely domesticated the Mylodon, it would still be around with its masters. More likely the animals were just rounded up in the open and chased into the cave, where they were kept alive with forage until the time came to kill and eat them.

Before finishing up with the current scientific opinion about the whole matter, one episode, amusing in retrospect, must be told. Early in this century Sir Ray Lankester, director of the Natural History Museum in London, permitted himself to be quoted to the effect that it seemed possible that a ground sloth of the Mylodon type might still be alive in little-known parts of Patagonia.

This was good enough for the owner of the London *Daily Express*. He decided to finance an expedition to Patagonia to search for a living Mylodon and bring it back to England, alive if possible, dead if it could not be helped.

The expedition was headed by a man named Hesketh H. Pritchard, who must have been an impatient type. Nobody knew at the time that Ameghino had blundered with respect to the *Iemish*, so Pritchard set out with what he believed to be a body of facts to guide him. In South America, he quickly learned that a major mistake had been made somewhere and he grew furious. Though he had traveled thousands of miles and had only another two or three hundred miles to go to reach Captain Eberhard's ranch, he did not do so. He turned around, went back to England and wrote perhaps the most ill-tempered book ever printed. The *Iemish* did not exist, the legend about it was the invention of some publicity seekers, the whole thing was a pack of lies and, most important, he, Hesketh H. Pritchard, had been hoaxed.

Well, how do things stand now?

One of the newer and most useful tools of science, radio-carbon dating, does not help much here for lack of material. The first list of radio-carbon dates (*Science*, February 2, 1951) contained two entries about giant sloth material. They were:

> No. 484 *Chilean Sloth:* Dung of giant sloth from Mylodon Cave, Ultima Esperanza, Chile (51° 35′S.). Not associated with human artifacts, though sloth and man found together in three caves 125 miles distant (*cf.* sample 485) 10,800 ± 570; 10,864 ± 720; 10,832 ± 400 (years).

> No. 485 *Chilean Bone:* Burned bone of sloth, horse and guanaco, associated with human bones and artifacts. Valuable in determining time of arrival of man at tip of South America. Material found in Palliaike Cave, 125 miles east of Mylodon. Comment: Most ancient of human samples from South America. 8639 ± 450.

In other words, the samples that happened to be dated are pretty old and do not help us in determining how long the giant sloth lived in South America. It would be so nice if we found a sample which at least makes it certain that Thévet's *Su* was a ground sloth.

Pritchard's expedition was not the last. Two others were organized. Both returned empty-handed. This, of course, is not proof that there are no living ground sloths any more; large portions of South America are still poorly known. And one can always argue that it is hard to see why a plant-eater should become extinct in green South America, where there have been no climatic changes for thousands of years. There is no answer to that argument except that no living, or freshly killed, ground sloth has yet turned up.

6

A Century of New Animals

TO BEGIN SOMEWHERE, let us consider an utterance of a man who was just about the most famous naturalist of his time, namely Georges Léopold Chrétien Frédéric Dagobert, Baron de Cuvier. He is called both the Father of Paleontology and the Father of Comparative Anatomy, and during his lifetime he was Titular Professor at the *Jardin des Plantes* (as the Paris Zoo is still misleadingly called), Chancellor of the University of Paris and a high government official of cabinet rank.

Georges Cuvier died 126 years ago, in 1832. Shortly before his death—say, around 1830—he said in the course of a lecture that the naturalists of the future would have to concentrate on extinct animals, since no new discoveries of large living animals were to be expected any more.

One might say that he was statistically right, even if he was wrong otherwise.

In the years since his death, several thousand species of extinct animals have been dug up and described, while only a few dozen large living animals have been discovered. And at first it must even have seemed as if Cuvier might be literally right, for two full decades went by without a noteworthy discovery. Then the "spell" was broken by the English traveler Hodgson who, in 1850, reported a new large mammal from Tibet.

It was the Takin (*Budorcas taxicolor*), also called the Gnu Antelope and best described as a very large and heavy mountain goat of dull brown color. It is rarely seen in zoological gardens, and if a garden does acquire one, the keeper is likely to be unhappy, for the Takin exudes a penetrating and offensive smell every minute of its life.

Some five years later, there came three more discoveries, all connected with the name of Père (Father) Armand David. The home of all three is China and they were vaguely known to the Chinese.

One of them was called *beishun*, which simply means "white bear" and which was said to live "in the mountains"— this being Asia, that term can cover a very large number of square miles. When Father David finally got hold of one, it turned out to be the Giant Panda (*Ailuropoda melanoleucus*); its cousin, the Lesser Panda, had been known for about half a century and was usually called Himalaya Raccoon.

The second of Father David's discoveries was a monkey. Its picture was known, because Chinese artists had painted it on vases and similar items. But it had always been thought to be just an artistic convention; a monkey with such a wildly colored fur and such a "little Lulu" nose obviously could not exist. Father David proved with skins and skeletons that it did and the scientific name became *Rhinopithecus roxellanae*, often referred to as the roxellana monkey or, sometimes, snow monkey.

The third discovery was even more unusual. Father David knew, like everybody else, about a walled-in Imperial Hunting Park near Peking. He also knew that no Chinese emperor had actually hunted there for centuries and that it was strictly forbidden to enter it. So one day he climbed the wall to see the animals inside.

Among herds of well-known game animals, Father David saw a large stag; he was sure that this animal was new to science. The Chinese called it *sse-pu-hsiang* which means "not like four" and is supposed to express the idea that the animal does *not* look like a stag, *not* like a horse, *not* like a cow and *not* like a goat. Another and simpler name, which became known later, is Milu.

Father David obtained antlers and skin—probably by bribing the guards; he never said how he did it—and sent them to Paris. A gift of live specimens was then arranged through diplomatic channels and Alphonse Milne-Edwards in Paris gave the scientific name *Elaphurus davidianus,* popularly known as Père David's Deer.

The subsequent history of Père David's Deer is one of those stories one would not believe if one read it in a novel. Père David's Deer existed *only* in the Imperial Hunting Park; it had become extinct everywhere else centuries ago. Then, in 1895, there was a flood and a famine and the hungry people ate all the animals in the Imperial Park. But a few specimens of Père David's Deer had been bought by the Duke of Bedford. They have turned into a large herd, so now the animal lives only in England (plus a few of the bigger zoological gardens).

At the same time when Père David's Deer was described in Paris, another new animal was described in England in the Proceedings of the Zoological Society. It was an antelope, the so-called Lesser Koodoo (*Strepsiceros imberbis*) which had lived unnoticed in East Africa.

Then there was a hiatus lasting just about a decade, until 1878, when another Englishman by the name of Waller reported a new gazelle from Somaliland. It was a rather small animal as far as the body went, but it had long legs, almost like those of a giraffe, and a fairly long neck. The scientific name at first became *Gazella walleri,* which was later changed into *Litocranius* ("small skull") *walleri.*

One year later, the zoological world became even more excited by a report from Russia. A Russian traveler, Nikolai Mikhailovitch Przevalski, reported that he had found a wild horse in Central Asia. Not a wild ass, which were known to exist in quite a number of places, not a feral horse (this is the term used for the wild offspring of animals), but actually a wild horse which not only had never been domesticated but had not even been known to exist. It was called *Equus przevalski* to the chagrin of all zoologists outside Russia, who have to learn to pronounce it as *Pshe-vall-skee*, with the accent on the *vall*.

Another wild horse entered the zoological scene only a few years later, in 1882. It was not really meant to be a discovery; it was intended as an international goodwill token. His Majesty, the Emperor Menelik of Ethiopia, gave it as a present to the president of the French Republic, whose name was Grévy. It turned out to be an unknown species of zebra, the largest of all living zebras, now known as Grévy's Zebra, or *Dolichohippus grevyi*.

In 1888, there came a shout of surprise from Australia. The discovery was physically small, but important. Australia is the continent of the marsupials or pouched mammals, but most of them were large enough and numerous enough to be quickly discovered. However, one had stayed unnoticed underfoot—literally. It was *Notoryctes typhlops*, the marsupial mole. Strangely enough, its fur is of a golden color of remarkable beauty.

The ostrich is, as everybody knows, the largest living bird, occurring normally in northern Africa. Its scientific name is *Struthio camelus*. In 1890, a German living in East Africa sent a live ostrich to the zoological garden in Berlin, with a note explaining that it had been caught on Masai territory. After a while, the experts felt that there was something somehow wrong and soon they put their finger on the "wrongness."

The African ostrich normally has a red or reddish neck and legs. That is the northern variety. The so-called Somali ostrich has a bluish-gray neck and legs. This one, though not of the northern variety, had a red neck and red legs. Moreover, the lower half of the long neck was covered with feathers, though normally the whole neck is nearly naked. It was a new species and was named Masai Ostrich, or *Struthio masaicus*.

One new bird seems to deserve another, and four years later a new and very large eaglelike bird was reported from the Philippines. It was said to eat mainly monkeys, which accounts for the scientific name of *Pithecophaga* (monkey-eater) *jefferyi*. (The name of the discoverer was Jeffery.)

Hard on the heels of the news of the monkey-eating bird came a chance discovery, made by the experts on board of the yacht of the then Prince of Monaco. The yacht was near the Azores, where local fishermen had just harpooned one of the toothed whales. The animal was too large to be handled by the fishing boats and the yacht offered its services for towing it ashore.

The whale was not quite dead and suddenly vomited the contents of its stomach, consisting mostly of torn pieces of large octopi. Among these pieces there was a damaged specimen of a seven-foot octopus that was completely unknown to science. It was named *Lepidoteuthis grimaldii* and none like it has been seen or caught since.

I am trying to tell of these discoveries in chronological order, but there are some difficulties.

There is a small mammal in Ecuador which measures 9½ inches on the average, of which 4½ inches are tail. It was first mentioned by R. F. Tomes in 1860 and he wrote that this would be a shrew if it did not have a rudimentary pouch. The trouble was that he had an immature specimen. In 1895, another specimen, adult this time, was found and described by the English zoologist Oldfield Thomas. It was a New World marsupial, closely related to extinct forms from Patagonia, and also related to other fossils which Georges Cuvier had found near Paris. Its name became *Caenolestes* which translates as "new robber," with reference to the old robbers of Cuvier.

If *Caenolestes* failed to impress the layman, the next discovery, made in 1900, certainly did. It was the Okapi, a short-necked relative of the giraffe which lives in the Congo Forest. Henry Stanley had heard of it some eight years earlier; the natives talked about a zebra in the forest. Zoologists snorted, for zebras do not go into the forest. By 1900, when pieces of skin came to London, it seemed that they had been wrong and that this particular zebra did.

Two years later, skulls and complete skins became available and the zoologists were proved right again—the animal was *not* a zebra and is not even striped all over. It had just happened that the striped portions of a cut-up skin had become known first.

The discovery of the Okapi (Fig. 23) was no doubt the greatest surprise since Father Armand David's finds. And Africa kept surprising zoologists.

Fig. 23. The Okapi.

First, in 1903, the Congo Giraffe came to light. It is only a "race," not a species, but still one should not think that a giraffe could have been overlooked for so long. One year later, a very large package arrived in London from Captain Meinertzhagen of His Majesty's East African Rifles, stationed in Kenya District. It contained an imperfect large black pelt and a perfect skull from another specimen. Quickly dubbed the Giant Forest Hog, it was new to science (though natives had told Stanley about it) and merely the very largest species of wild pig in existence. Its scientific name became *Hylochoerus meinertzhageni*. A grown male measures six feet in length.

In 1910, one more antelope was discovered by Buxton in the southernmost portion of Ethiopia. It was named *Nyala buxtoni*.

During the same year, a rumor from the Far East was confirmed. On the small island of Komodo, situated between the somewhat larger islands of Sumbawa and Flores, "dragons" had been rumored to live. In a manner of speaking, the rumor was true—it was *Varanus komodoensis*, the largest of the generally large monitor lizards. The biggest actually measured was 11 feet 8 inches long, but the natives said that larger ones had occasionally been taken away.

In the last year of the First World War, another unknown mammal was reported from China for the first time, but because of war and revolution, not much attention was paid to it at the time. It was a dolphin, but one living in rivers. Its name became *Lipotes vexillifer* and even now not much is known about it.

There followed a comparatively long pause of nineteen years, but then the year 1937 brought two discoveries, one from Asia and the other from Africa.

The Asian discovery was nothing less than a species of wild cattle, the Kouprey (*Bos sauveli*), which had somehow managed to live unnoticed in Indochina; probably often seen, sometimes shot, but unrecognized as a scientific novelty.

The African discovery was a bird and it was by no means a chance discovery. One of the "okapi expeditions" had brought, among other things, a bundle of bird feathers acquired from natives of the Congo region by trade.

This bundle of feathers reached New York in 1915 and Dr. James P. Chapin of the American Museum of Natural History sorted them out at leisure. He could determine the origin of all the feathers but one, a rather large one which just would not fit any known bird.

Years later, in 1936, Dr. Chapin found in the Congo Museum in Tervueren (near Brussels) in Belgium two stuffed birds. They were labeled "young peacocks," but actually they were unknowns. However, they bore feathers like the one that could not be classified. Next year, Dr. Chapin shot the bird in the Congo district. It was the Congo peacock (*Afropavo congensis*), which had been familiar to the natives under the name of *itundu*.

The Congo peacock is not even especially rare!

If the Congo peacock was discovered by a systematic search, the next discovery was pure chance. It was the fish now known as *Latimeria,* a very strange fish indeed, a so-called *coelacanth* which was rather well known as a fossil. But everybody was convinced that this type had become extinct some 50 million years ago. Then one was caught by a fishing vessel off the South African East Coast in December 1938. It remained the only one for many years and the blame for the failure to find more was squarely put on the Second World War.

Now we know that the zoologists had looked in the wrong area. The first Latimeria had been caught off East London, which is a considerable distance to the south of Madagascar. For reasons not known, it had strayed nearly 2000 miles from its home grounds, which are the waters around the Comores Islands between the African coast and the *northern* tip of Madagascar.

Even around the Comores Islands, this fish from the distant geological past is not frequent. Still, it is frequent enough for the islanders to have coined a special name for it—*conbessa*. Since this is French territory, the whole Latimeria case is in French hands, which are indubitably capable but, one suspects, a bit slow. When I wrote a column on Latimeria in GALAXY (May 1956), it was stated that a four-volume monograph on this fish was forthcoming. It still is.

Though Latimeria might be said to be the most important discovery of that century of new animals, it is not the end of the story.

In 1950, the German zoologist Dr. Ingo Krumbiegel identified a new animal from its skin. It is a mountain wolf living in the South American Andes. Presumably the people who shot it—one South American dealer is said to have had four skins at one time—thought these were feral dogs. It has yet to be taken alive.

And two birds were "re-discovered," which is to say that they were found to be still alive, even though the books said they were extinct. One was the Bermuda Çahow, the other the large and beautifully plumaged Takahe (*Notornis*) of the South Island of New Zealand.

Originally the Takahe had lived all over both the North and South Islands of New Zealand, but that was before white explorers, missionaries and settlers arrived. By about 1800, though the North Island form was extinct, the somewhat different South Island form was known to be still alive.

As time went on, a few specimens came to light, all from the vicinity of Lake Te Anau, which lies inland of the New Zealand fjord area of the South Island. The "last" Takahe was killed by a dog on August 7, 1898. Fortunately the owner of the dog saw at once what it was and saved the specimen for a museum.

However, enough rumors about bird footprints came out of the area so that, in November 1948, Dr. Geoffrey E. Orbell led a small expedition to the mountains to the west of Lake Te Anau. Suddenly they saw a Takahe. One member of the expedition threw a net to catch it and caught two. They were tied up to be photographed and then released again. Now the Takahe, like the Bermuda Cahow, is strongly protected by law.

I know that I am now expected to go and make a few predictions of what might still be discovered. I will, but before I do so, a quick look at some statistics ought to be most instructive.

The first book that tried to systematize all living animals was the *Systema naturae* of the Swedish scientist Karl von Linné, better known by the Latinized version of his name: Carolus Linnaeus. The tenth revised edition of his book (published over 200 years ago, in 1758) is always taken to be *the* edition of the *Systema naturae* and listed 180 mammals, 450 birds, 400 fishes and, of the insects, 600 beetles, and not quite as many different moths and butterflies.

In 1900, no less than 3500 mammals were known (this included so-called geographical variations), 13,000 birds, 5000 reptiles and amphibians, and about 30,000 fishes. Among the insects, they counted in 1900 an almost even 100,000 *Lepidoptera* (moths and butterflies), 30,000 *Hemiptera* (leaf hoppers, bugs, etc.), 130,000 *Coleoptera* (beetles), 30,000 *Diptera* (flies, etc.), 40,000 *Hymenoptera* (wasps, bees, *et al.*), 13,000 *Odonata* (dragonflies) and so on and so forth. There were 20,000 different spiders known, 8000 worms, 50,000 molluscs (snails, etc.) and 3000 echinoderms like starfish.

A few years before this count was taken, the Prussian Academy of Science, well supplied with money at the moment, decided to produce a modern equivalent of the *Systema naturae*, reflecting the zoological knowledge at the turn of the century. They worked bravely, producing 60 volumes of zoology. Then they had to give up because one of their mem-

bers, the zoologist R. Hesse, calculated that the completion
of the work would take 270 years—provided that no new discoveries would be made during that time!

As regards predictions, let's start with the easiest place of
all, the oceans. We *know* that there are unknown fish; they
have been seen through the window of the bathysphere by
William Beebe. They haven't been taken yet, but they
will be.

Then, also in the oceans, there is the problem of the Great
Sea Serpent which might be a mammal.

Thirdly, there seems to be a hitherto undiscovered long-
necked and large marine turtle.

Taking the continents one by one, nothing specifically is
rumored from North America. South America has many rumors emanating from it, but none specific enough to start
theorizing. For a while, a kind of hunt was on for surviving
giant sloths, but that has died down. Though South America
will probably provide a number of novelties in time, there
is no way of guessing what they might be. Europe can also be
very nearly written off, except for a persistent rumor about a
fairly large unknown lizardlike animal in the Austrian Alps.

Africa is a different story. There are rumors in quantity
and they might very well be true.

One is usually referred to as "Nandi bear" (also as *chimiset,
nunda* and *mngwa*—don't ask me how this should be pronounced), which probably is not a bear but a man-killing
mammal, possibly feline.

The other is a river- or lake-dwelling killer of hippopotami,
referred to as the *chipekwe*, or *mokéle-mbêmbe* and, possibly,
lau. What can be learned always has a few things in common
—the unknown animal lives in fresh water, but can go on
land. It kills hippopotami, but does not eat them. It has a
long neck. And somehow the impression of a reptilian nature
is conveyed.

Passing on to Asia, the main mystery and possible next discovery is the *yeti* or "abominable snowman" whom the Sherpas describe as being the same size they are (average 5 ft. 6 in.) and covered with long-haired but very thin fur of a brownish color. It is possible that this is actually a very primitive human race. Elsewhere, primitive races have been pushed by their less primitive neighbors into environments that the less primitive peoples did not want themselves. This may well have happened in Central Asia to a primitive and somewhat peculiar-looking human type.

In Australia, there is one unknown animal that may be said to be almost known. It has been seen repeatedly in the northeast part of Australia, the Cape York Peninsula. It is rather matter-of-factly described as a "cat," as large as a strong medium-sized dog, with a head resembling that of a tiger. It is described as striped, black on gray, with sharp claws and pointed ears. One witness saw it kill a kangaroo.

The animal is obviously rare and its habitat restricted to a comparatively small area. It could be either a real "cat" from the description, a feline carnivore like a large lynx. Or else, which would be much more interesting if it turned out to be the case, it could be a marsupial carnivore like the Tasmanian Tiger.

New Zealand, finally, could harbor two more discoveries that would not be complete novelties because they have been rumored for so long. One is the Waitoreke, the only (but undiscovered) indigenous land mammal of New Zealand. The other, rumored from the Dusky Sound area, not too far from Takahe country, is a small Moa, the type called by scientists *Megalapteryx*. Like the Takahe, this *Megalapteryx* was known to the Maori and the most recent Moa remains known are of this type. Whether there are any left is doubtful, but not impossible.

Well, that's the story. Like all stories of discovery, it has no end, properly speaking, because the end consists of opening new vistas.

7

Largest of Their Kind

SOME TIME AGO, I received a letter, not from an individual but from a whole high-school class in Kansas, asking for an article on the question of which mammal, bird, reptile, fish and so forth is the largest in its class, past or present. When I started looking things up, I began to realize—as you will in a little while—that Kansas was as logical a place as Hollywood to ask this particular question. Kansas may not have any extremely large animals to offer at this moment, but it certainly is a state with a gigantic past!

To begin somewhere, let's start at the top, with the mammals. The largest land mammal of the present period is, by a comfortable margin, *Loxodon africanus*, the African elephant. An old bull will stand 11 feet tall and reach a weight of from six to eight tons. If one can put full trust in the reports of big-game hunters, bulls standing 11½ feet tall have been shot in Africa, but I'd feel much happier about these reports if the trophy had ended up in some museum where a measurement can be repeated in case of doubt. At any event, the African elephant is, on the average, half a foot taller and a ton heavier than the nearest runner-up, which is, of course, *Elephas indicus*, the Indian elephant.

In the not-too-remote past, however, it would have been the African elephant who would have been designated as runner-up. No, *not* to the mammoth—at least not to the Siberian mammoth, which was smaller than the Indian elephant. But one European variety of mammoth, found in Austria and now on exhibition in the Natural History Museum of Stuttgart, topped the African elephant by 30 inches, and another variety of extinct elephant, *Elephas trogontherii*, found in southwest Germany near Wiesbaden, topped this giant by another 10 inches.

Even this super-elephant, though, was not the largest land mammal of the past. The record, as far as present knowledge goes, is held by *Baluchitherium grangeri*, a "hornless rhinoceros" from the Tertiary period of southern Asia, which was 27 feet long and stood around 18 feet tall. The present Indian rhinoceros could have walked under a standing Baluchitherium without ducking.

But mammals do not live on land only. The marine mammals of today hold the record not only over the land or marine mammals of the past, but also over everything else that ever moved, including the dinosaurs.

The largest whale is probably the kind called the Blue Rorqual, *Balaenoptera sibbaldii* (or *B. musculus*). Even conservative naturalists grant this monster a body length of 80 to 85 feet. (Statements that can be found in print go as high as 101 feet.) The weight of a fully grown specimen of this whale is estimated to be close to 150 tons. Even if this should be wrong by a couple of dozen tons or so, the large whales of today are considerably heavier than brontosaurus, which is calculated to have weighed in at 38 tons on the hoof. The whales of the geological past, being far smaller than those of the present, would take at best fourth or fifth place.

Proceeding to the birds, one at once gets into the dilemma of what to go by, linear dimensions or weight. The bird with the largest wing-spread of the present time is the Wandering Albatross, the *albatros errante* of the South Americans or *Diomedea exulans* of the ornithologists. The largest ever measured had a wing-spread of 12 feet and weighed 15 pounds. The condor, both South American and Californian, comes close with a maximum spread of just about 11 feet, but it weighs as much as 31 pounds. In the recent past, there was an even larger California condor that topped the wingspread of the albatross and was probably heavier, too, than the existing type.

Naturally, the flightless birds are the biggest, for ground installations always weigh more than airborne equipment. The largest of today, the African ostrich, may look down at you from a height of eight feet and weigh 160 pounds.

Only a few centuries ago, however, the African ostrich would have been runner-up to several other bird giants.

The biggest of the New Zealand moas, *Dinornis maximus*, was not a lot taller (probably just a matter of inches), but must have weighed more than twice as much. This moa was certainly still alive in 1600, the date for which the giant ostrichlike bird of Madagascar is mentioned as still living, though only by hearsay, not from personal observation of the reporter.

The Madagascar bird, *Aepyornis ingens*, stood 10 feet tall. It was of lighter build than *Dinornis*, but it did lay the biggest bird egg known to science—almost 14 inches long, with a cubic content equal to that of 7 ostrich eggs or 185 eggs of the kind that come by the dozen.

The largest—or, rather, most massive—of extinct birds well known to paleontologists was *Diatryma gigantea*, from the lower Eocene of Wyoming. This heavy bird, possibly related to the cranes of today, had a skull almost 20 inches long, with a beak to match. Some seven feet tall when standing erect, it must have weighed well over 300 pounds.

We now come to the reptiles and there, as everybody knows, the past greatly outshines the present. But the present is not doing as badly as most people think.

The large Indian crocodile, *Crocodilus porosus*, which shows a most remarkable preference for salt water and long swims in the ocean, would not look too much out of place in a Cretaceous landscape. One specimen, of which the skull is in the British Museum, has been measured by Boulenger and found to be 33 feet long, with a circumference of 13 feet 8 inches!

The largest living turtle is a hefty animal, too. It is the leatherback turtle (*Dermochelys*) of the high seas, which grows to an overall length of nine feet, the carapace measuring 6½ feet, and the weight of such a giant is an authenticated 1450 pounds.

The largest living snake is the South American anaconda (*Eunectes murinus*), of which many a wild tale has been told. Zoologists usually say that this snake will reach a length of "well over 20 feet" and generally will be willing to settle for 25 feet as the limit. But one reputable source mentions a specimen that measured 30 feet. However, it was measured after death (understandably so) and if you stretch a dead snake of such length for measuring, you may add one or two feet to its "live length" without meaning to.

The largest lizardlike reptiles of today are, of course, the monitors. The East Indian *Varanus salvator* grows to a length of 10 feet, while the still larger *Varanus komodoensis*, from the small island of Komodo in the Sunda Sea, is two or three or maybe even four feet longer. Both are very long-tailed, so that these figures are slightly misleading. The heaviest Komodo monitor actually weighed was just about 100 pounds.

Although all these are respectable figures, they shrink by comparison with reptiles from former geological periods. The one exception is the Indian crocodile. I don't know of any extinct true crocodile that grew as big. But the monitors are just small leftovers. Only some 20,000 years ago, Australia had a monitor lizard that was more than 20 feet long and may have reached 30 feet.

The largest extinct reptiles were the sauropod dinosaurs of the type of the well-known brontosaurus. Diplodocus was probably the longest because of an elongated tail; measurements lie between 70 and 75 feet from nose to tip of the tail. Not longer, but more massive by far, and probably the heaviest of the dinosaurs was *Brachiosaurus brancai* from the Upper Jurassic period of East Africa (Fig. 24). The length of the humerus (bone of the upper arm) of Brachiosaurus is 84

Fig. 24. Brachiosaurus Brancai. Upper Jurassic of East Africa.

inches, as compared to 47¼ inches for the same bone in Diplodocus. Brachiosaurus could still breathe while walking along the bottom of a 40-foot-deep lake!

The largest leatherback turtle would also look quite small next to *Archelon ischyros,* from the Upper Cretaceous of

Kansas. This marine turtle of some 60 million years ago must have been 13½ feet long when alive and heavy in proportion, presumably around 3500 pounds. Its armor had been somewhat reduced for the sake of mobility, but there is little need for armor in a turtle with a three-foot skull and a beak like a guillotine.

For company, *Archelon* had 20-foot mosasaurs, swimming reptiles with four big paddles, a flat tail and long teeth.

Above the waters where Archelon and the mosasaurs competed for fish, the largest flying animal of all Earth's history wheeled on leathery wings, also looking for fish. This was *Pteranodon ingens*—mostly wings, with a ridiculously small body and legs, but with a large though paper-thin skull and a long sharp beak. The wing-spread of Specimen No. 2514 has been computed at 26 feet 9 inches.

The amphibians of today are generally small. A 10-inch salamander is "big" and a two-pound toad something worth mentioning. Still, in Japan there lives a salamander, called Hanzaki and Hazekoi by the Japanese, which grows to slightly over five feet in length. This is *Megalobatrachus maximus*, the Japanese giant salamander that was discovered about 1825 by the German traveler von Siebold and caused a small sensation in scientific circles in its time—not only because it is the largest living amphibian, but also because it was the first case of an animal having been known in fossil form before being discovered alive.

To find really large amphibians in the geologic past, we have to go back to before the dinosaurs to encounter the labyrinthodons, so named because of the strange construction of their teeth. One especially familiar but exceptionally badly named species was *Mastodonsaurus acuminatus*, from the Triassic of northern Europe, with a three-foot skull and an overall length of about 12 feet.

The fishes are another class where the present holds its own well as compared to the past, even though it has to be admitted that the record-holders belong to an ancient type—namely, the sharks. The basking shark (*Selache maxima*) is known to reach a length of 30 to 35 feet, while the whale shark (*Rhineodon typus*), recently made famous by Thor Heyerdahl and his Kon-Tiki expedition, is well established with 45-foot specimens, and even 60 feet has been tentatively accepted as a possible maximum size.

Past geological periods have not yet furnished anything larger than the whale shark among the extinct fishes. A possible exception is a fossil shark called *Carcharodon megalodon*, from the Miocene of the Vienna area. Only the teeth are known so far, and if the size of the shark was in proportion to the size of these teeth, it might have been larger than *Rhineodon*.

Now don't dismiss the invertebrates as tiny. True, they usually are, for a one-inch beetle will be considered a big fellow and a six-inch earthworm "enormous" and the African snail *Achatina fulica*, which the Japanese spread over a large number of Pacific islands as a food supply during the Second World War, is known as the "giant snail." Its shell is five inches long and its overall length nine inches; it is the second largest of the land snails of our era. (The largest, also African, is about a foot long.) But there are a number of other impressive exceptions from the rule that most invertebrates are small.

The largest clam of our time—and of the past, too, as far as is known—is *Tridacna gigas*, which occurs near the Philippines, on the Great Barrier Reef of Australia and generally in that area. It can reach a size of five feet and a weight of 500 pounds. Its virtually indestructible shells were brought to Europe for centuries and were often used as basins for holy water in small churches, especially in Bavaria and Austria. "Two-thirds of my class should make excellent naturalists; they have been baptized from Tridacna shells," a south German zoology instructor once said to me.

The largest molluscs are the giant squid, the *Kraken* of the Norse, but unfortunately nobody can give any definite figures. One killed by the crew of the French corvette *Alecton* in 1861 could not be actually measured, since the crew of the ship, although they tried hard, failed to hoist it aboard. But the monster was directly alongside the ship, so that a good and reliable estimate could be made—50 *feet without the tentacles!*

No giant fossils of a comparable type are known, but armorless octopi would hardly fossilize. They would be eaten by a large variety of marine creatures before mud or sand could cover the body. However, some octopi produce shells the way the living nautilus does and such shells fossilize easily. You can see long rows of these *ammonites* in every museum.

The largest known is, so to speak, a childhood friend of mine. "I knew him well," of course, long after its discovery. The enormous thing was found in a quarry at a place named Seppenrade in Westphalia in 1895. Since *pachys* (Greek) means "thick," it was promptly christened *Pachydiscus seppenradensis*. The diameter of the shell is 8¼ feet. The weight of the fossil, more precisely a *steinkern* or internal mold, is 7700 pounds. And the octopus that grew it lived during the Upper Cretaceous period.

Even something as unlikely to be gigantic as a jellyfish can grow to enormous size. At Nahant, Mass., Prof. Louis Agassiz measured one in which the bell was 7½ feet across and the tentacles more than 120 feet long! In the southern Pacific, one kind seems to grow to a diameter (without tentacles) of three to four feet as a rule. At that size, it weighs about 90 pounds.

A twelve-foot earthworm may sound as unlikely as a 90-pound jellyfish, but such earthworms exist in Australia. They have as many as 500 segments and are fairly thin when extended, about ½ inch. The handbook I consulted states that the only bird known to eat these earthworms is the Australian laughing kingfisher. I can add one other—I saw a photograph of a domestic duck swallowing hard but successfully. Yet this is not the longest worm by any means. The "broad fish tapeworm" will reach a length of 60 feet, with a width of ¾ inches! But a parasite is obviously a special case.

When it comes to insects, one has to ask, of course, "what kind?" The largest living butterfly is a moth and so are the runners-up. The record is held by the South American owl moth with a span of 11 inches. The south Asiatic Atlas moth measures 10 inches in wing-spread, but has much wider wings than the owl moth. Our North American species do not compare too badly, the cecropia moth reaching 7½ and the polyphemus moth 6½ inches.

Among the beetles, the elephant beetles of South America and the goliath beetles of Central Africa run in very close competition, both being four inches long in good specimens. The hercules beetles of tropical America measure up to 6½ inches in length, but much of this is just the long projecting horn. In actual length, a "walking stick" from Borneo probably wins with 11 inches, but it is quite thin.

How about the insects of the past? In the far remote past, the Carboniferous period, insects like dragonflies were the largest. The biggest present-day dragonflies, from tropical America and Borneo, span between 6½ and 7 inches maximum. *Titanophasma*, from the Carboniferous of Europe, had a wing-span of 18 inches. For quite some time, it was thought to be the largest, but then *Protodonata* with a 2½-foot spread was found in the Permian of Kansas.

Crustaceans and, in general, arthropods still have to be mentioned. When the New England coast was first reached, stories of lobsters of incredible size went back to Europe. One famous natural history book of the sixteenth century, by the municipal physician of Zurich, Dr. Konrad Gesner, even contains a picture of a 6-foot lobster eating a man. Gesner stated that this is what he had been told, but neither he nor his artist had seen a lobster of such size.

The fact is that the American lobster runs larger than the European lobster and that old specimens reach considerable size. The largest really established measured 23¾ inches and weighed 34 pounds.

In sheer size, a spider crab from the Japan Sea, *Macraucheira kaempfferi*, surpasses this lobster, since it stilts along over the ocean floor on legs spanning six feet. Its body, though, is not much larger than a fist.

The largest arthropod known became extinct some 450 million years ago. It thrived during the Silurian period and is known to science as *Pterygotus*. The overall length was nine feet; it belonged to a completely extinct group called the eurypterids. We don't know whether they lived in fresh water or salt water. But they were obviously carnivorous and the terror of anything smaller that happened to come within reach.

And there you have a condensed record of the giants of the past and present. Incidentally, Man rightfully belongs on this list. Despite those who insist on viewing him as small and puny, he actually is a member in good standing of the one per cent or less of the Earth's total life population that can be called giants! Figure it out for yourself—he averages 5½ feet in height and 130 pounds (extremes are 8½ feet and 600 pounds) with an arm-spread of 5 to 8 feet. What's small about that?

8

A Pangolin Is a Pangolin

THE CURATOR OF A SMALL COLLEGE museum once produced some amusement for himself and his students in the following manner: He took a mounted specimen of a pangolin, removed the labels and put it all by itself in a display case in a prominent position. On Sunday, when the museum was open to anybody, a few students with index cards and pencils stood at the display, and every visitor who looked at it was handed an index card and asked to write down his opinion about the nature of the object displayed. The cards were then put through the slot of a suggestion box without comment. After the doors had closed, the curator unlocked the box, and he and his students read and sorted the cards.

Total count was 81 and the "vote" ran as follows: 36 visitors had written "lizard" or "tropical lizard"; 11 had guessed at a rare type of alligator (one had stated "alligator from Ecuador"); 15 had written "small dinosaur"; 8 had said that it was some kind of armadillo; 4 thought it was a man-made object and one had guessed that it might be a large pine cone. Precisely half a dozen had known that it was a pangolin.

What is a pangolin?

The first answer is that it is a mammal, just like you and me, or our cats. The overall length of a fully grown specimen is between 3 and 4 feet, depending on the species. It may be added at this point that all observers who saw pangolins in the open for the first time expressed surprise about its agility.

The animal which, when dead and mounted, has a decidedly "wooden" look, can run fast and climb trees, sometimes hanging by its tail only.

The next question, logically, is where one would have to be to see a pangolin in the open. Quite a number of different places would do—for the pangolins, though nowhere numerous, have a wide distribution. Four species inhabit Africa, and three more live in Asia. But before we look at the distinctive characteristics of the different species a few general statements must be made. While the outstanding characteristic of the pangolins are the scales, they have hair too. The hair grows between the scales and on the underside; in old specimens the belly hair has often been worn away so that the tough skin is exposed. As a rule a female pangolin produces only one offspring at a time. The young is fairly large and always shows an exceptionally long tail, even in those species that are not very long-tailed when grown. One interesting point is that the newly born pangolin has just as many scales as it will ever have. As it grows larger, the individual scales grow larger, too, but their number does not increase.

One reason why pangolins are rarely seen is that they are nocturnal. For the better part of the day they sleep in burrows they dig quickly with the enormous claws of their front feet. Since one can find numerous burrows even where there are only a few pangolins around, it seems that they simply dig a new burrow when they feel like sleeping and do not bother to return to the burrow they slept in before. But captive specimens did not seem to mind shifting the sleeping schedules; they were willing to be up and around even in bright sunlight if food was provided.

Now for the different species. For a long time it had seemed natural to divide the pangolins into two families: the African pangolins and the Asiatic pangolins. But in about 1890 Professor Paul Matschie of the Berlin Society of Naturalists began a thorough study of all the known pangolins and came to the conclusion that all seven species form only one family, regardless of habitat. Because Matschie did such a thorough job, his classification is still in use. Beginning with the African species we have:

(1) *Manis tetradactyla* (originally named *M. longicaudata,* which means "long-tailed") with a tail much longer than the body. It has broad scales forming a point, the hairy portions of the body are dark brown in color. It is a very agile climber, as is the next species,

(2) *Manis tricuspis* which is also long-tailed. The hairy portions of the body are white, however, and the scales are narrow, the largest of them forming three points, hence the name.

(3) *Manis gigantea,* up to five feet long, is not a climber but a fast runner when needed. Its tail is only as long as the body and is pointed. The lower part of the forelegs is covered with scales, not with hair as in the first two. These three species live in tropical West Africa; the fourth African form,

(4) *Manis temmincki* (Fig. 25) lives in South Africa and the southern portions of East Africa. It is not a tree climber but an animal of the steppes. The tail is only as long as the body but very heavy with a rounded point.

The three Asiatic species are:

(5) *Manis pentadactyla* of India and Ceylon. The claws of its hindlegs are *much* smaller than those of the front legs. The center row of the scales on its tail runs all the way to the tail tip, but on the underside the tail has a clearly defined spot where the skin is exposed. This is assumed to be a tactile organ.

(6) *Manis aurita* lives in Burma, Hainan and Formosa. The claws of its hind feet are also much smaller than those of the front feet, but the scales on the sides of the body and those of the hindlegs show a definite keel, which is missing in the case of *M. pentadactyla.* The seventh member of the family is

(7) *Manis javanica* of the Malay Peninsula and Indonesia. It has keeled scales like *M. aurita,* but the claws of the four feet differ only slightly in size, though those of the hind feet are still somewhat smaller. It is a tree climber, which may be the reason why it is less well known than the other pangolins.

Fig. 25. Manis temmincki. *The pangolin of the South African plains.*

Except for *Manis temmincki,* which was discovered by a Dutch traveler by the name of Smuts some ninety years ago, the pangolins came to the attention of European naturalists at an early period. References in old works are rare and, when there are any, they are short. Evidently the writers said nothing since they did not know what to say. This procedure of keeping quiet where there was no story was all right for books that just intended to acquaint the reader with the diversity of creation but it would not work if you wanted to be systematic. The great Swedish systematizer of both plants and animals, Carolus Linnaeus, at one time had to meet the challenge offered by the pangolins.

Systematizing is more than just description. It involves, among other things, the question of relatives. When it came to animals like the various wild oxen life was easy for Linnaeus; their common characteristics could not be overlooked even if one should try. The same went for the dog-like animals and for horses, asses and zebras. But what were the characteristics the pangolins shared with other mammals? The scales? Well, the beaver has a scaly tail, but the beaver was very obviously a rodent like rats, mice and squirrels. The pangolin, equally obvious, was not. It was one of those misfits that explorers had brought home from various points of the earth.

The aardvarks of Africa were misfits of the same kind, they did not seem to be related to anything else. Then there were the armadillos of Central and South America, and the sloths and, last but by no means least, the giant anteater.

Looking over this collection of animals that stood apart from all the others with such determination, Linnaeus suddenly saw something that could be used. The pangolins were completely toothless. So was the giant anteater. The armadillos do have teeth, but they are small and useless. The sloths do have strong teeth, but very few of them. There was a common characteristic—a comparative or complete lack of teeth.

Linnaeus may have felt faint doubts himself, but a classification has to be finished at some time, so he decreed the order of the *Edentata* ("the toothless ones"), and he finally had a place for aardvarks, anteaters, armadillos, pangolins and sloths.

Naturalists that came after Linnaeus were not completely happy with his *Edentata* but for about a century the classification was left alone. It was only during the latter part of the nineteenth century that some anatomists declared that Linnaeus had gone by something that was unimportant. The "order" was taken apart into three. One comprised all the pangolins and the pangolins only, and it was named *Pholi-dota*, from the Greek *pholidotos* which means "armored with scales". The South American forms, the anteaters, the sloths (plus the then recently discovered giant sloths) and the armadillos (with their extinct relatives, the glyptodons) were left together as the *Xenarthra*, the "strange-jointed ones."

Fig. 26. Manis pentadactyla. *The pangolin of India and Ceylon.*

The African aardvarks were put separately into an order named *Nomarthra* from the Greek word for "roaming."

There were other attempts. The giant anteater, the aard-varks and the pangolins share a preference for the same kind of food, namely termites (ants as well as termites in the case of the pangolins) and have developed the same method of eating. All three have long, slender and sticky tongues which they dangle into a cluster of termites so that the insects stick to the tongues. Then they pull their tongues in and swallow the catch. A few naturalists seriously suggested of grouping these three into an order of "worm-shaped-tongued animals" even though they have absolutely nothing else in common. It was as bad as the *Edentata* of Linnaeus, fortunately the majority of experts refused to go along with this. The other classification at least had the advantage of declaring the pan-golins on the one hand and the aardvarks on the other to be isolated survivors from the past, not related to anything living.

Well, if the pangolins are not related to anything living, how about their relationship to extinct forms.

In other words, then don't fossils give some indication about their evolution?

The answer, unfortunately, is a straight "no". In the first place fossil pangolins are rare. In the second place the few fossils we have don't help.

The whole Tertiary Period is subdivided into five subperiods with a total duration of about 55 million years. The first of these subperiods is called the Paleocene, with a duration of about 5 million years. The following subperiods, named Eocene, Oligocene, Miocene and Pliocene shared a total duration of about 50 million years in about equal measure. Between the end of the Pliocene subperiod and the present there is only the Pleistocene (total duration about one million years) with its extensive glaciations.

Now let's see what we have as far as pangolin fossils are concerned.

There are some very poor remains from the Eocene of France and the Miocene of Bavaria, that is from areas where there are no pangolins at present. All that is proved by these remains is that pangolins did live in Europe during the Tertiary Period. Better fossils were found in India. One from the Pliocene subperiod has been named *Manis sindiensis*; if this form were still alive it would simply constitute the eighth member of the family. Another fossil from the Pleistocene of South India is identical with the living *Manis gigantea* of western Africa.

Evidently the pangolins split off from the other mammals prior to the Eocene subperiod, possibly as early as the Cretaceous Period. They are an ancient tribe that acquired its special characteristics about 60 million years ago, and they haven't changed since then.

Since we cannot trace how the pangolins acquired their special features it remains to describe them. Not all their characteristics are unique, their tongues, as has been mentioned, have parallels in the tongues of the anteater and the aardvarks. Their enormous digging claws are shared with those of the aardvarks and, to some extent, with those of the armadillos and the anteaters.

But two characteristics are unique.

One of them is the very obvious scales.

The other is a construction of the stomach which is such that professors of zoology and of anatomy usually have to stress in their lectures that they are not indulging in some obscure scientific joke but are merely telling the truth. The fact is that the pangolins do have teeth, but in their stomachs.

But let us take the scales first.

The early naturalists like Linnaeus simply accepted them. They were an unusual feature to be sure, but there they were, they could be touched and counted. It was after Darwin and because of Darwin that others began to wonder whether they were true scales. In fact, because of the theory of evolution one was almost compelled to doubt that.

The ancestors of the mammals had been reptiles, and reptiles often have scales, though no reptile can sprout hair. The great innovation of the mammalian body was a mechanism for maintaining a constant temperature in the body. The mammalian body produced heat, and in order to avoid excessive heat losses an insulator had to be grown, a fur of some kind. Now it seemed logical that the mammalian skin that could grow hair had exchanged this ability for the ability to grow scales. Hence the scales of the pangolin had to be something that only *looked* like scales. Maybe the hairs grew in flat tufts and some kind of skin secretion made them stick together to produce imitation scales.

But if this were true, the pangolins should be born with a fur and one should be able to see the scales form. However, the newly born foot-long pangolin already has all its scales.

Fortunately this was a point that could be checked by dissection and the German zoologist Professor Max Weber, after carrying out such studies, stated his conclusion in no uncertain terms. "The scales can definitely be compared to the scales of reptiles, and the differences between this armor and that of the reptiles is only the difference that exists between the two kinds of skin, mainly the one that reptiles periodically shed their skins. In the case of the pangolins the losses that are caused by abrasion are covered by continued re-growth . . . the derma of the pangolins forms papillae that are folded over pointing in the direction of the tail. The papillae are covered by epidermis that turns into a horny substance, forming the scales." The way these scales grow explains why they can be erected and can also be moved laterally to some extent.

Of course it is still true that the mammalian skin, as a rule, has lost the ability to grow scales. The pangolins are just an exception to that rule. The skin of their ancestors retained the ability to grow scales, but it was also able to grow hair. As a matter of fact, the pangolins even grow two kinds, ordinary hair between the scales and on the belly, and hairs that have special blood sacs around their roots at the tip of the mouth.

And now we come to the unique construction of its stomach. The principle with virtually all mammals is that the food is mechanically broken up by the teeth in the mouth. The stomach then goes to work on this mashed and saliva-coated food and does so by chemical means only. Reptiles lack teeth that can mash food; at best they can tear it into small pieces. The stomach of a reptile, therefore, has a much harder job and it is interesting to note that many of the larger reptiles swallow pebbles so that there is some mechanical mashing inside their stomachs.

It has been mentioned that two other kinds of living mammals eat insects in the same manner as the pangolins, by using their long and sticky tongues as traps: the South American anteater and the African aardvark. But in spite of its name the giant anteater does not eat ants but only termites, and the aardvark does the same. Termites are soft-bodied.

The pangolins eat termites *and* ants, and they seem to prefer ants. Since there are no teeth in the mouth the ants are swallowed whole, and the method of catching them makes it inevitable that sand grains and small pebbles arrive in the stomach along with the hard-shelled ants, many of which must still be twitching. This sounds like a most indigestible mixture. And it would be for any other stomach, but the pangolin stomach is built for it. It works with mechanical and chemical means at the same time.

At the entrance to the stomach the stomach walls are equipped with a hard horny skin that can exert considerable pressure and grinds up the ants and sand grains almost like millstones. In the center of the stomach the gruel of now crushed ants and saliva is attacked by stomach acids and other chemicals. As if this were not thorough enough the area that leads from the stomach to the intestine has another grinding mechanism in readiness, this time consisting of horny knobs that even look like teeth.

And this completes the picture of this creature, an animal that sprang from unknown ancestors more than 60 million years ago, with the bodily organization of a higher mammal, the scales of a reptile, the habits of an aardvark, the tree-climbing ability of a squirrel and with a stomach like nothing else.

It isn't a lizard, tropical or otherwise, nor a small dinosaur. It is neither a work of art nor a pine cone. It isn't even an armadillo. It is in a category of its own. It is a pangolin.

9

Hunting the Dodo

ONCE UPON A TIME, there lived on the island of Mauritius a bird named the dodo, with the scientific name of *Didus ineptus.*

Come to think of it, this* is not a good beginning. The story of the dodo is not a fairy tale but the truth, or as much truth as can still be established. Moreover, this first sentence is a very unscientific oversimplification. Let's try to make it a bit more accurate. Then it will read just about like this:

From a period, the beginning of which cannot be ascertained, but which might be considered roughly equivalent to the beginning of the glacial age in higher latitudes, until about the year 1680 A.D., a large and flightless bird, classified as being the representative of a sub-order of the *Columbiformes* or pigeonlike birds, known to have existed on the island of Mauritius, or Zwaaneiland, also known as Ile de France, was called dodo, or dodaers, or dronte, but also *dinde sauvage*, *Walchvogel* or *gekapte Zwaan* (hooded swan) and several other names, with the scientific designation of either *Didus ineptus* or *Raphus cucullatus*, which are equivalent in scientific usage, but with *Raphus cucullatus* holding the chronological priority.

Well, now, this is more accurate.

It also complies with the order drilled into newspapermen: "Get all the facts into the first paragraph."

But I'm very much afraid it would probably be most intelligible to somebody who knows these facts already and who, logically, does not have much reason to read it at all.

I had better start over again, this time with the fundamentals. To the east of Madagascar, strung out along the 20th parallel of southern latitude, there are three reasonably large islands.

Their current names are Réunion, Mauritius and Rodriguez —at least, that's the way the name of the last appears on Admiralty charts, both British and American. For some unfathomable reason, the dependency of Rodrigues, when it makes an official report to the colony of Mauritius, spells its name with an "s" at the end. I am making a point of this difference in spelling for the sole reason that it happens to be the smallest of all the difficulties and discrepancies we are going to encounter. The more serious problems will come up later.

It is hard to say just who discovered these islands. There exists at least one old map on which the three islands have Arabic names. It is quite likely that Arab trading vessels did discover them, but without paying any special attention to their discovery, since the islands were uninhabited and it is exceedingly difficult to barter on uninhabited islands.

At any event, the Arabs did not even bother to locate the islands with any degree of care. On the map mentioned, they are drawn as forming an equilateral triangle and are placed far too close to Madagascar.

The first European discoverers were Portuguese but, strange to say, it was the second of the Portuguese discoverers who had his name attached to the islands.

The first one was Diogo Fernandes Pereira, who sailed these waters in 1507. On February 9th of that year, he found an island some 400 miles to the east of Madagascar which he named Santa Apollonia. It must have been the present Réunion. Soon after, his ship, the *Cerné*, sighted the present

Mauritius. The navigator landed and named the island after his ship, as Ilha do Cerne.

This, I might say right here, led to two different misunderstandings. Much later, around the middle of the nineteenth century, somebody who obviously did not know the name of Pereira's ship wondered why the navigator should have named the island after the island of Cerne, mentioned by Pliny the Elder. Wherever Pliny's Cerne was located, it could not be to the east of Madagascar.

The other misunderstanding took place quite soon after Pereira's voyage. Dutch explorers who came to Mauritius and knew the old name thought that Cerne was a miswriting for *cigne* (swan) and that Pereira had thought the dodos to be swans. The Dutch did not bother with the zoological problem involved; they "translated" Diogo Pereira's name into Dutch as *Zwaaneiland*.

Pereira, who was on his way to India, found Rodrigues later in the same year. It was first named Domingo Friz, but also Diego Rodriguez. The Dutch apparently found this hard to pronounce and talked about Diego Ruy's island, which then was Frenchified into Dygarroys—but the official French name for a time was Ile Marianne.

Six years later came the second discoverer, Pedro Mascarenhas, who visited only Mauritius and Réunion. No name change was involved for Mauritius because of this rediscovery, but Santa Apollonia (Réunion) was renamed Mascarenhas or Mascaregne, and to this day the islands are called the Mascarene Islands.

The subsequent history of the islands was just about as complicated as this beginning. Réunion, the largest of the three islands, 970 square miles in extent, was officially annexed to France in 1638 by a Captain Goubert from Dieppe.

I don't know why one annexation was not considered sufficient, but the historical fact is that the annexation was repeated in the name of Louis XIII in 1643 and once more in

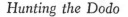

Manu Adriani Venny Pictoris.

Fig. 27. *The dodo of Mauritius as sketched by Adrian van de Venne in 1626.*

1649 by Etienne de Flacourt, who changed the name from Mascarenhas to Ile Bourbon. After the French Revolution, that name had to go, of course, and Réunion was re-established. But then history can be read quite easily from the various changes, for it became Ile Bonaparte. Since 1848, it is again Réunion.

Considered non-politically, Réunion is a volcanic island with three rather tall peaks. The tallest is the Piton des

Neiges, which measures 10,069 feet. The other high elevation
is simply called Le Volcan by the inhabitants of the island,
but Le Volcan has more than one peak. One, called Bory
Crater, is 8,612 feet above sea level and extinct. The other
crater, known as Fournaise, is only 8,294 feet tall but still
active.

An island in such a location can grow tropical fruit and
there are banana plantations and breadfruit trees, not to mention coconut palms. But these plants were introduced. The
original vegetation included a dwarf bamboo, a variety of
casuarina trees and a plant called by the trade name "red
tacamahac," botanically *Calophyllum spurium.*

The second island, Mauritius, is somewhat smaller than
Réunion (about 720 square miles) and likewise of volcanic
origin. But all volcanic activity on Mauritius is a thing of the
fairly distant past. The names of its three highest mountains
reflect the changing ownership of the island through the centuries. The highest one, 2711 feet, is called Black River
Mountain. The second one, 2685 feet, is Mt. Pieter Botte,
while the third, 2650 feet, is called Pouce.

The island is surrounded by coral reefs which a ship's captain has to know well, but it has a fine natural harbor. These
two features prompted the Dutch to annex it in 1598 and they
gave it its current name after Count Maurits of Nassau.

The Dutch abandoned Mauritius in 1710. For slightly more
than a half a century (1715-1767), it was French and called
Ile de France. In 1810, it was taken by the English, who
restored the Dutch name.

Right now, Mauritius is a "spice island" where spices,
pineapple, mangoes, avocados and bananas are grown, along
with sugar cane. But the original vegetation is still represented
by ironwood trees, ebony trees, traveler's trees and bamboo.
Of course, domesticated animals were introduced on both
islands, but Mauritius is somewhat special even in that re-

spect—the deer that can be found there came from Java, not from Europe.

As regards Rodriguez, its story is similar but shorter. Its extent is only 43 square miles. It is volcanic in origin, with 1300-foot Mt. Limon as its highest peak, and there is a fringing coral reef. The ownership of the island was Dutch, French and English in succession. In all cases, the first inhabitants were either deportees or people in voluntary exile, some of them mutineers, some refugees from religious intolerance.

Though all this had to be mentioned to establish a background, none of these facts would have made any of these islands famous. The only one which would enjoy a kind of restricted fame would be Mauritius, among stamp collectors, because of an early philatelic error which produced some of the rarest stamps in existence. But these Mascarene Islands are famous because they once were the home of the dodo and related birds.

The story of the dodo (let's concentrate on the Mauritius dodo for the time being) looks rather simple, if somewhat sad, in rough outline. Its existence was first reported by Dutch navigators, who were far less thorough in their descriptions than one would now wish they had been. But they made up for this to some extent by bringing live specimens back with them to Europe. There they were painted, mostly by Dutch painters and, again it must be said, not as well as one would now wish.

But the major blunder was committed in England. About 1637, give or take a year, a live Mauritius dodo arrived in England. It lived there for quite some time, and after its death, it was "stuffed" (badly, no doubt) and found a place in Tradescant's Museum in London in 1656. A few decades later, the stuffed dodo was transferred to the Ashmolean Museum at Oxford. This was in 1683—as we now know, two

years after the last report of a live dodo on Mauritius was put
on paper by one Benjamin Harry.

In 1755, the curator of the Ashmolean Museum decided
that the moth-eaten old skin was a disgrace to his fine collection and ordered that it be thrown away to be burned
with other trash. At the last moment, somebody wrenched
off the head (partly decayed) and one foot (in good condition). They are now about the rarest items on record.

Even this outline story contains one more surprising item.
The first scientist to include the dodo as an exotic bird in a
book on natural history was Carolus Clusius in 1605. Later,
Carolus Linnaeus gave it a scientific name, and quite natu-
rally the dodo entered into the zoologicals works of Buffon in
France and Blumenbach in Germany.

But by 1800, nobody had ever seen a dodo. The available
paintings did not seem convincing. They looked like caricatures to begin with and did not even agree with each other.

Some scientists, bent on a housecleaning in scientific literature, began to doubt whether there had ever been such a
bird. Maybe it was all a misunderstanding, if not worse, and
the descriptions had meant the cassowary.

At any event J. S. Duncan of Oxford felt obliged, in 1828,
to write a paper with the title: "A summary review of the
authorities on which naturalists are justified in believing that
the Dodo, *Raphus cucullatus* (*Didus ineptus*), was a bird
existing in the Isle of France, or the neighbouring islands,
until a recent period." Mr. Duncan can be said to have saved
the dodo from secondary extinction in scientific literature.

But let's go back now to the original sources. The first man
to write about the dodo was the Dutch Admiral Jacob Cor-
neliszoon van Neck, who went to Mauritius with eight ships.
Four of them returned to Holland in 1599, the other four in
1601. Admiral van Neck's narrative appeared in Dutch in
1601 and translations into English, French and Latin were

printed during the same year, a German translation one year later.

In spite of this volume of printed matter, there are still a number of question marks. The original journal, presumably written on shipboard, was enlarged for publication—we don't know whether by the admiral himself or by an editor. Moreover, one old naturalist, who did not leave Europe, gave a dodo picture which, he said, was copied from Admiral van Neck's journal. But this picture cannot be found in any known edition of the journal.

The passage in the admiral's journal in which the dodo is first mentioned reads:

> Blue parrots are very numerous there [referring to Mauritius] as well as other birds; among which are a kind, conspicuous for their size, larger than our swans, with huge heads only half covered with skin, as if clothed with a hood. These birds lack wings, in the place of which three or four blackish feathers protrude. The tail consists of a few soft incurved feathers which are ash-colored. These we used to call *Walghvogels* for the reason that the more and the longer they were cooked, the less soft and more insipid eating they became. Nevertheless, their belly and breast were of a pleasant flavor and easily masticated.

The Dutch word *Walghvogels* (also spelled *Walchvogels*) translates literally as "nauseating birds," but it led to one of the many mistakes that crowd the dodo's short life history.

About two hundred years later, it was asserted in German books that there had been Forest Birds, so named, on Mauritius. There probably were, and still are, forest birds on Mauritius, but the Forest Bird was only a sloppy translation, appearing in its German form of *Waldvogel*. Spelling in those days was helter-skelter in any language, so somebody probably thought that "walgh" was just a poor rendering of "Waldt," a then frequent spelling of the German word *Wald*, which means forest.

Since this has raised the problem of the name of the bird, it might be just as well to clear up this additional difficulty as much as possible.

In the most recent specialized professional work on the dodo, by the Marquis Masauji Hachisuka, not less than seventy-nine different names are listed. But the confusion is not quite as large as this figure seems to indicate, for the names clearly fall into a small number of classes.

One set of them tries to be descriptive. They are mostly French, as, for example, *austruche encapuchonné* (hooded ostrich), *cygne capuchonné* (hooded swan) and *dinde sauvage* (wild turkey). Another set are either translations or mistranslations of Dutch names. The Dutch names themselves are either variations on the theme of *walghvogels* or else descriptive terms similar to the French names just mentioned.

Just two words emerge as, so to speak, "exclusive" terms. One is the name *dodo*, with the variations *dodaars* and *dodaerts*, and the other one is *dronte*.

It is reasonably certain that "dodo" is a name coined by the Portuguese, as witness a letter written in 1628 by Emanuel Altham about "very strange fowles called by ye portingals Do Do."

The fact that Altham pulled the two syllables apart, thereby changing their pronunciation, is "very suspicious-making," as a French lady I know phrased it. It is so suspicious—or, rather, indicative—because old Dutch and German writings spell the name as *doedoe* and *dudu*, all of which must be pronounced "doodoo." Since it has no real meaning in *any* language, it can well be, as has been asserted, an imitation of the bird's call.

The Dutch variation *dod-aars* or *dod-aers* is rather clear to an English speaker, especially in view of the Dutch descriptive remarks *ende heeft een rond gat* ("and has a round rump," as van Neck put it) or *rond van stuiten* ("round of stern," as Capt. Willem van West-Zanen wrote in 1602).

However, the name dronte, which in Dutch and in German was used about equally frequently as dodo, still is not explained. The Englishman H. E. Strickland, who wrote the first book about the dodo in 1848, and it is still good, accepted the explanation that this term was coined by Danish sailors, using their verb *drunte*, which means "to be slow." This is not only somewhat far-fetched on the face of it, for the Danes, for a change, have not contributed anything to the story of this bird; it is not even necessarily correct. We simply don't know whether the dodo was slow and the evidence is not very much in favor of this assumption.

The Dutch zoologist Prof. A. C. Oudemans—yes, the man who wrote the 600-page book on the Sea Serpent—has pointed out—in another book devoted to the dodo only—that there was a now obsolete Middle-Dutch verb *dronten*. Its meaning was "bloated" or "swollen," which sounds much more reasonable. But Prof. Oudemans could not prove that this was actually the derivation; a lot of early writings on the dodo seem to be lost.

The records are incomplete also as regards the number of birds taken away alive. If it were not for a chance mention in Peter Mundy's journal—he served with the East India Company from 1628 to 1634—we would never know that two of them were brought to India. But his statement is definite: "Dodoes, a strange kind of fowle, twice as big as a Goose, that can neither flye nor swimm, being Cloven footed; I saw two of them in Suratt [the first British settlement in India, started 1612] house that were brought from thence [Mauritius]."

There is a similar chance mention about one having been sent to Japan, but Japanese scientists have failed, in spite of much effort, to trace its fate from Japanese chronicles and books.

Going by such remarks on the one hand and, on the other hand, by sketches and paintings stated or reported to have been made from life, Dr. Hachisuka listed a total of twelve specimens of the Mauritius dodo as having arrived in Europe: one in Italy, two in England and nine—five males and four females—in Holland.

In other books, particularly in works which treat the paintings as paintings instead of as ornithological illustrations, larger figures are usually mentioned. This is partly due to counting sketches and paintings made from earlier paintings. Mostly, however, it is due to the fact that no distinction is made between the gray Mauritius dodo and similar birds from the other two Mascarene Islands.

But no list, whether of specimens or of paintings, can be considered final. In 1914 and 1915, a German scientist, Dr. S. Killermann, set out on a systematic dodo hunt in museums, libraries and art galleries and discovered about half a dozen pictures that had simply been overlooked before. Killermann's feat could probably be repeated by somebody today with the inclination and the necessary time and money.

As has been mentioned, the Clusius picture has been copied from a lost original of van Neck's journal. Somebody might still find it. Similarly, it is known that an unnamed artist on board of one of the ships commanded by Admiral Wolphart Harmanszoon made several drawings from life while the ship was in Mauritius harbor in 1602. The originals are now "lost," but somebody might find them.

Likewise, one of the several oil paintings of dodos made by Roelandt Savery is listed as lost.

In short, while a dodo investigation is no longer virgin territory, it is still a fertile field with possibilities for a diligent researcher.

One of the earliest and best pictures of a Mauritius dodo drawn from life is the pen-and-ink drawing by Adrian van de Venne. It was made in 1626 and shows a male. This is what we now think of as the normal appearance of the dodo. However, it was Prof. Oudemans who first realized that the dodo must have had two "normal appearances"—one fat stage and one gaunt stage. This assumption explains many old sketches which look like caricatures; the latter impression is considerably strengthened by the fact that a number of sketches were made while the birds were moulting.

Oudemans' idea makes it possible to arrange all these sketches in a logical sequence, pre-moulting, at the height of the moult, post-moulting, fat and gaunt. But why a bird on a tropical island, where the food supply should be more or less the same all year round, should go through a gaunt stage at regular intervals is not yet fully explained.

The Mauritius dodo became extinct between 1681, the last time it is mentioned as living, and 1693, the first time it fails to appear on a list of the animals and birds of the island made on the spot. By 1750, the people living on the island did not even know any more that there had been such a bird.

A hundred years later, there lived a man on Mauritius who was an ardent naturalist. This man, George Clark, not only knew about the dodo, but was determined to find dodo remains. They had to be somewhere on the island, for the entire species could not possibly have become extinct without leaving traces. But where would these traces be located?

At first glance, the situation did not look too promising. "In fact," George Clark wrote, "there is no part of Mauritius where the soil is of such a nature as to render probable the accidental internment of substances thrown upon it. It may be classed under four heads: stiff clay; large masses of stone forming a chaotic surface; strata of melted lava, locally called *pavés*, impervious to everything; and loam, intermixed with fragments of vesicular basalt—the latter too numerous and too thickly scattered to allow anything to sink into the mass by the mere force of gravity. Besides this, the tropical rains, of which the violence is well known, sweep the surface of the earth in many places with a force sufficient to displace stones of several hundred pounds weight."

After having reached this point, Clark all of a sudden had a new idea. If these tropical rains swept everything before them, where did they sweep it? Well, there was a kind of delta formed by three rivers running into the harbor of Mahébourg. If dodo bones had been washed into one of the rivers, this was the likely place where they might have come to rest. One part of that delta was a marsh known locally as *le Mare aux Songes*. Mr. Clark promised himself that he would dig there, as soon as he had the time and some means to pay laborers for the actual work.

About 1863, he began to dig, finding large numbers of dodo bones at the very bottom of the marsh, to the delight of anatomists, and to the intense astonishment of aged Creoles who were standing around and were somewhat annoyed by seeing something on their own island which they had not known about. As a result of George Clark's successful digging, there is no doubt about the dodo's skeleton. As a matter of fact, it was this material which helped to unravel such problems as were posed by the sketches of artists who did not know anatomy—at any rate, not bird anatomy.

And while no museum can have an authentic dodo, several museums can, at least, boast authentic dodo skeletons, like the one at the Smithsonian Institution which was put together by Norman H. Boss.

The American Museum of Natural History in New York has such a skeleton, too, but it also has something which makes casual visitors wonder whether a dried skin might have survived somewhere.

The museum has a restoration, made in the taxidermy studios of Rowland Ward in London. The feet and the head are copied from the preserved specimens. The feathers are those of other birds, correct in color and, as far as can be ascertained, correct in shape. The dodo is in the fat stage, the one we know best from pictures.

Other Islands, Other Dodos

ABOUT 130 MILES OF OPEN SEA separate the two islands of Mauritius and Réunion. This is not a long distance for birds with a reasonable power of flight and it is only logical that many birds are common to both islands and even to Madagascar. For a flightless bird, however, 130 miles of open sea might as well be 3,000 miles—it could no more cross the one than the other. Hence it is obvious that the Mauritius dodo, of which Peter Mundy said specifically that it "can neither flye nor swimm," could not cross over to Réunion. Nor could a flightless bird of Réunion cross over to Mauritius.

Logically, then, if there also was a dodo on Réunion, it could not be expected to be the same as the dodo of Mauritius. Similar, yes, but only that. Their ancestors, presumably still capable of flight when they somehow got to the Mascarene islands, were no doubt the same. But even a short separation, as geologists speak of time, would produce very noticeable differences.

Well, there *was* a dodo on Réunion and it *did* differ from the Mauritius dodo, but for more than a hundred years, naturalists did their best to overlook this difference. Yet the very first witness pointed it out. He was an Englishman by the name of J. Tatton who, in 1625, published an account of a voyage made a dozen years earlier under Captain Castleton.

Reporting on Réunion, he wrote: "There is a store of Landfowl, both small and great, plentie of Doves, great Parrats, and such like; and a great fowl of the bigness of a Turkie, very fat, and so short-winged that they cannot flie, being

white, and in a manner tame; and so are all other fowles, as
having not been troubled or feared with shot."

The only other witness who saw the Réunion dodo on the
island and wrote about it was the Dutch traveler Willem
Ijsbrantszoon Bontekoe van Hoorn. He spent three weeks
there in 1619, and not only described what is unmistakably
a dodo, but even referred to it as a *Dad-eersen*. Unfortunately, he did not say anything about its color.

Later researchers, though, kept coming across pictures
which did not jibe with the other dodo pictures. Not only
was the plumage white with yellow wing feathers, but they
were different in other respects, too. The feet were more
slender, the tail was different and so was the bill.

Now it is true that there are sketches of the Mauritius
dodo in which the bill looks different, the reason being that
the moulting dodo also shed the sheath of the bill. But these
white dodos seemed to have their sheath in place. The pictures are all by just two artists, Pieter Holsteyn (around
1640) and Pieter Withoos (around 1685). Since it is most
unlikely that a full-grown specimen would live for forty-five
years in captivity, this indicates that two specimens of the
white dodo reached Europe.

The older naturalists failed to draw a clear distinction and
even H. E. Strickland, in his monumental work on the dodo
(1848), did not do so.

The white dodo was introduced to science as a distinct
species as late as 1907, when the Hon. W. Rothschild published his work *Extinct Birds*. (It had the subtitle: "An attempt to unite in one Volume a short Account of those Birds
which have become extinct in historical Times, etc.," but the
short account turned out to be in folio with no less than 45
color plates.) The scientific name proposed for it was *Didus
borbonicus*. In 1937, Dr. Hachisuka changed the scientific
name (for various reasons that do not interest us here) to
Victoriornis imperialis.

Fig. 28. Sketch of the White Dodo of Réunion, by Pieter Holsteyn, early seventeenth century.

Probably because Réunion is more mountainous than Mauritius, the white dodo lived longer than the gray dodo. There is a report that Mahé de la Bourdonnais, when he was governor of both islands, sent one to France. There is no record from the other end—we don't know whether it got to France or not—but Mahé de la Bourdonnais was governor from 1735-1746, long after the Mauritius dodo was extinct.

The Réunion dodo fails to be present for the first time in a survey made in 1801. It must have succumbed to dogs, rats and pigs during the latter half of the eighteenth century. That there was still something else to be said about Réunion was not even suspected until recently. But this additional mystery can best be explained with a detour to the third of the Mascarene islands, Rodriguez.

As has been told in the preceding issue, the island was first reached by the Portuguese Diogo Fernandes Pereira in 1507.

It took almost two centuries until settlers got there, and even these went to Rodriguez only as a second choice.

They were French Huguenots who were supposed to go to Réunion from Holland. It was a small group of only eleven men. Their chosen leader was a man a few years past fifty at the time whose name was François Leguat. His younger brother was also in the group.

The Dutch ship, with the French Protestants aboard, left Holland on September 4, 1690, and arrived at Réunion on April 3 of the following year. What happened then is not quite clear, but it seems that it had been believed in Holland that the French had abandoned the island. When the ship's captain realized that they had not, he did not land but set course for Rodriguez, where the French stayed for about two years. Then they built a boat and sailed for Mauritius.

A weird and senseless odyssey was the result of this act. About half a year after they had landed, they were discovered by the governor who, after a few months of deliberation, banished them to a small rocky island offshore. There they were kept prisoners for three years and then shipped, still as prisoners, to Batavia. A year later, they were released and sent back to Holland as free men, where they arrived in June, 1698.

François Leguat did not stay long, but went to England, where he rewrote the journal he had kept all along for publication. In 1708, both Leguat's French original and an English translation appeared.

Other voyagers had said before Leguat that there were "dodos" on Rodriguez, but Leguat was the first man who had lived there for any length of time. Moreover, Leguat could draw. He provided illustrations for his book and there can be little doubt that he had made the sketches on the spot, because some of them are rather complicated maps and plans.

LE SOLITAIRE

Fig. 29. *The Solitaire of Rodriguez, as pictured in François Leguat's book of 1708. Drawing probably by Leguat himself.*

"Of all the Birds in the Island," the English edition read, "the most remarkable is that which goes by the name of *Solitary,* tho' there are abundance of them. The Feathers of the Males are of a brown grey Colour: the Feet and Beak are like a Turkey's, but a little more crooked. They have scarce any Tail, but their Hindpart covered with Feathers is roundish, like the Crupper of a Horse; they are taller than Turkeys . . . The Bone of their Wing grows greater towards the Extremity, and forms a little round Mass under the Feathers, as big as a Musket Ball. That and its Beak are the chief Defence of this Bird. 'Tis very hard to catch it in the Woods, but easie in open Places, because we run faster than they . . . Some of the Males weigh forty-five Pounds."

Leguat reported that the males were brown in color, the females either brown "or fair, the colour of blonde hair"; most likely the brown ones were older females. He also mentioned that the females had a "head-band, like the head-band of Widows, high upon their Beak," and that lighter feathers on their chest formed an outline like the bosom of a woman. Leguat's drawing, therefore, is that of a female, since the males lacked these characteristics.

There is no other drawing of a solitary besides Leguat's. However, just as in the case of the Mauritius dodo, remains of the solitary have been excavated on Rodriguez, so that a few nearly complete skeletons could be constructed.

Again the story has a few wrinkles which were added later.

In 1761, one of the famous transits of the planet Venus across the face of the Sun was due to take place and Rodriguez happened to be in such a geographical position that a fine observation of the transit could be made from there. The man to go to Rodriguez for this purpose was Abbé Pingré. In addition to doing the astronomical job for which he had taken the trip, Abbé Pingré reported that the solitaries were still around. He is the last man to have seen them.

Some five years later, Pingré's colleague and compatriot Le Monnier decided that the expedition should be honored in some manner. He had discovered a number of small stars in the space between the constellations Libra, Scorpio and Draco which could be put together into a new constellation. He was going to call it *Solitarius* to honor Pingré, Rodriguez and the transit of Venus expedition.

But he needed a picture of the solitary, and since his compatriot Brisson had recently published an enormous book on birds, he felt sure that it would be in there. Looking through the entries, he found a *solitaire* listed and copied the picture onto his star map. I don't know whether Le Monnier ever learned that the picture he used was that of *Turdus solitarius,* the solitary thrush!

The other wrinkle is tied up with the name of Geoffroy Atkinson, a professor of Romance literature who has written several books with titles like "The Extraordinary Voyage in French Literature before 1700," "The Extraordinary Voyage in French Literature, 1700 to 1720" and so forth. Personally, I failed to be enchanted by them; they are solid work, but I had the impression that Atkinson knew literature and nothing else.

Now I learn from Hachisuka that Atkinson, in 1921, went overboard with his interest in extraordinary voyages and declared that Leguat never traveled! He could "trace" every item in Leguat's journal to its "sources." The account of the Cape of Good Hope came from this book, the sea turtles from that book, the story of his imprisonment from still another book, the building of a boat from somebody else's memoirs.

One biologist who read this began to wonder. Leguat had said things about the anatomy of the solitary which were correct, as the skeletons proved, but which could not be found in any other book.

Fig. 30. *The gable stone of Veere on Walcheren, discovered by Prof. Oudemans.*

While the biologist was still brooding over the article, two French librarians very politely requested that Atkinson answer a few simple questions, to wit:

Fig. 31. Female Réunion solitaire, picture discovered by Dr. S. Killermann.

If Leguat had never rounded the Cape of Good Hope, why do the archives of Cape Town tell about the ship, its arrival, departure and so forth, all with the same dates as given by Leguat? Then, if Leguat never saw Rodriguez, why does the earliest map of the island (other than Leguat's own) name a few places after him? Why are there official reports from Mauritius telling of the arrival, imprisonment and deportation of refugees from Rodriguez? And, finally, why is there correspondence with the fleet commander about the trip to and return from Batavia?

Well, Atkinson did accomplish one thing. Before him, nobody had doubted the authenticity of Leguat's journal. Now we are sure that it cannot be doubted.

It remains to tell the scientific name of Leguat's solitary. It is *Pezophaps solitarius*. The first of these two names is put together from two Greek words: *pezós*, which means "pedestrian," and *phaps*, which means "pigeon."

Some readers who know something about the dodo's story may have wondered why I did not quote some of the well-known source material about the subject. For example, Sir Hamon L'Estrange's account in his memoirs:

> About 1638, as I walked London streets, I saw the picture of a strange fowle hong out upon a cloth and myselfe with one or two more then in company went in to see it. It was kept in a chamber, and was a great fowle somewhat bigger than the largest Turky Cock, and so legged and footed, but stouter and thicker and of a more erect shape, coloured before like the breast of a young cock fesan, and on the back of dunn or dearc colour. The keeper called it a Dodo, and in the ende of a chymney in the chamber there lay a heape of large pebble stones, whereof hee gave it many in our sight, some as big as nutmegs and the keeper told us that she eats them (conducing to digestion), and though I remember not how far the keeper was questioned therein, yet I am confident that afterwards shee cast them all again.

My reason for not bringing this up earlier is that this statement almost certainly does *not* refer to the dodo, even though the keeper called the bird by that name. The coloration does not fit the gray Mauritius dodo and certainly not the white Réunion dodo. Nor does the "more erect shape" as compared to the turkey.

As Dr. Hachisuka points out emphatically, this is a description of a bird of the type of the solitary, not of the dodo type. It must have been the use of the name dodo which made earlier researchers accept Sir Hamon's account as one of the dodo and to surmise that this was the specimen which later was in Tradescant's Museum and finally thrown away.

There have always been some descriptions of a bird from Réunion which did not quite "fit."

There was the narrative of a Frenchman named Carré who went to Réunion in 1668: "I saw a kind of bird in this place which I have not found elsewhere: it is that which the inhabitants call the *Oiseau Solitaire*, for, to be sure, it loves solitude and only frequents the most secluded places; one never sees two or more together; it is always alone. It is not unlike a turkey, if it did not have longer legs."

Another very similar description came from the Sieur Du-Bois who arrived in Réunion in 1669. He listed the birds he saw, and when he came to *Solitaires*, he stated: "These birds are so called because they always go alone. They are as big as a large goose and have white plumage with the tips of the wings and tail black. The tail feathers are like those of an ostrich, they have a long neck, and the beak is like that of the Woodcock, but larger; the legs and feet are like those of a turkey."

Carré's and especially DuBois' statements led Strickland to suspect that maybe Réunion had both a dodo and a solitary.

Rothschild, after weighing all the evidence, also said that there must have been two different birds on Réunion, either two kinds of dodos which were quite far apart in appearance, or else one dodo and one solitary resembling the Rodriguez type.

A. C. Oudemans, ten years after Rothschild, took the position that all this was a mistake. The men who reported on them probably were not too observant as regards the moulting stages of the birds. Oudemans' main argument is that nobody described both birds, so to speak, side by side.

This is admittedly sad, yet it so happens that nobody did. But if you read what reports there are, you get the impression that the bird called *solitaire* seems to have been quite numerous, while the white dodo obviously was not. Moreover, Réunion is large enough so that the two birds could have had different habitats.

Somewhat ironically, Prof. Oudemans himself produced evidence for a solitary in addition to the one on Rodriguez.

During the First World War, Prof. Oudemans, vacationing with his wife, looked at the gable stone of a house in Veere, on the island of Walcheren. The stone said that the bird pictured was an ostrich. It also clearly gave the date: 1561. Oudemans did not need long to see that the bird, whatever it was, was not an ostrich. But it could be a dodo. If so, this was the earliest dodo picture on record.

The picture is reproduced here. Prof. Oudemans sent me a print in 1936 when we had correspondence mostly about the Loch Ness animal.

It must be a gaunt dodo, Oudemans felt, for it certainly could not be a Rodriguez solitary. Leguat had been very specific about its being tailless with a round feather-covered rear end. Look at the tail feathers, Oudemans wrote. Almost like those of an *Afrikaansch struys* (African ostrich) or like those of a dodo.

Well, the answer is that it was not a Rodriguez solitary but a Réunion solitary (now called *Ornithaptera solitaria*) and the tail feathers, so prominent on the old Dutch gable stone, are just as prominent in the so-called dodo of Florence, one of the pictures discovered by Dr. S. Killermann. This picture is now taken to portray a male Réunion, while another picture, also discovered by Killermann, shows a female. Comparing this picture with the one of a Rodriguez female by Leguat, one can see how the two birds resembled each other and in what respects they differed.

There is one more picture of the same bird (not reproduced here) which is now at McGill University in Montreal. It is of Italian origin, being picture No. 29 in the so-called "Feather Book" made by Dionisio Minaggio in Milan in 1618. It consists of 156 large pictures with birds, practically all of them hunting scenes.

The interesting point is that the birds are never painted. The real beaks, feet and feathers of birds have been used. Unhappily, the picture of the Réunion solitary is "faked." That is to say that legs and beak have been painted and that the feathers used for the body are those of other birds. But it is undoubtedly the same bird as a dodo of Florence.

That attempts to ship Réunion solitaries to Europe were made is stated by Carré, who says that two of them were caught to be sent to the king (of France) but aboard ship they died of "melancholy." In a few other cases, shipment must have been successful. The 1561 stone masonry in Holland must have had a model. One male must have arrived in Italy around 1618. We do know that there was one on exhibit in London around 1638 and there is evidence that a female got to Vienna in or about 1657.

The story has a postscript called the dodo of Nazareth or, more learnedly, *Didus nazarenus*.

I thought the case had been nicely cleared up by Iosif Kristianovitch Hamel of the Russian Imperial Academy of Science in St. Petersburg, which published a fairly long study in its Bulletin of the Physical-Mathematical Section in 1848.

Professor Hamel, after reading all the sources, had found a convincing piece of evidence. You remember that the Dutch called the dodos *Walghvogels* or "nauseating birds" because their taste was so atrocious. (One of them declared firmly that the dodo was for wonder, not for food.) The French had translated *Walghvogels* correctly into *oiseaux de nausée*. But one François Cauche, who spent two weeks on Mauritius in 1638, wrote about the dodos *nous les appellions oiseaux de Nazaret*.

Cauche probably did not try to taste dodo and did not see why the birds should be nauseating, so he thought that the word *nausée* was actually *Nazaret*, which sounds somewhat similar in French. And there was a place called Nazareth nearby on a nautical chart. There still is, but it is now labeled a "bank" while on earlier charts there is an island by that name. Professor Hamel thought this was a simple mistake.

He may be right. But when Prof. Oudemans checked old charts systematically, he found a few in which the name of Nazareth is not placed next to an island where we know that there is no island, but near the existing, if tiny, island which on modern charts appears as Ile Tromelin.

Nobody knows much about Ile Tromelin. It cannot be of any importance because the latest edition of the Admiralty Charts states that its position may be five miles off on the map. If it were of any importance, this would surely have been ascertained by now. Maybe the mapmakers who produced the old charts seen by Oudemans simply lettered Nazareth next to it because there was supposed to be such a place and it was the only island left in the whole area, the other suspected islands having turned into banks and shoals.

But Oudemans said that *Didus nazarenus* cannot be dismissed completely until Ile Tromelin has been carefully investigated. Not that he expected to find live dodos of any kind; he meant subfossil remains like those found on Mauritius and on Rodriguez.

In principle, Oudemans is naturally correct; as long as there is an uninvestigated lead left, the book should not be closed.

No such investigation has taken place. But until it is and the facts prove otherwise, I prefer to accept Prof. Hamel's explanation.

10

The Last of the Moas

I HAVE THE FAINT FEELING that the word "moa" would be far less known than it is if it were not such a useful word for crossword-puzzle purposes. No statistics are available—as so often happens in the case of cultural items of probably undisputed value—but I would guess that a diligent researcher could turn up a different crossword puzzle for every day in the year which shows three spaces to be filled in with something defined as "extinct bird."

To the naturalist, the three letters M-O-A spell something else again—it might as well be D.O.A. Exploring and literate men got to New Zealand too late to see the moas, just as they have been too late in quite a number of other places. To make the whole story more lamentable, exploring seamen occasionally did get to such interesting places in time.

But they did not know what to look for, from our point of view. Maybe they simply missed what we would consider interesting. In some cases, one may suspect that they merely failed to write down what they saw. At any event, a modern naturalist, transported back to earlier but still historical times by time machine, could seize on various lost opportunities.

He would have joined the Phoenician sailors, for example, who set out in 596 B.C. to round Africa at the request of Pharaoh Nekho (or Niku) and who actually succeeded in doing it during the two years that followed. We don't know whether they passed through the channel separating Madagascar from the African mainland or whether they sailed "out-side" of Madagascar. We do know that they made numerous landings; one of them may have been on Madagascar. If a modern naturalist had been along, he would have made sure of such a landing in order to look for the near-fabulous *Aepyornis*, the enormous ostrichlike extinct bird of that island.

We don't really know how it looked. Of course we can reconstruct its skeleton; in fact, we have. But we have no idea of its plumage. All we know is that it has not been extinct for very long. The Phoenicians of that trip would surely have found it; even the Crusaders might still have been in time.

A modern naturalist would also accompany the Arabs who at a reasonably early time sailed the Indian Ocean and did go as far east as Sumatra and Borneo. The modern naturalist would have talked the shipmaster into turning due south there to get to the Australian shore. Presumably he would have been in time to see the now extinct giant marsupials of Australia, colossi as large as the strongest bull. They were no longer among those present when Australia was actually discovered.

Such a naturalist might even have seen the *Megalania*, indubitably preferring a safe shelter if this occasion came up. The *Megalania* was a monitor lizard of which the following things are certain: it was enormous in size and did not become extinct until fairly recent times.

As to its size, learned opinions differ—some scientists felt that the animal might have been more than thirty feet long; others gave it only twenty feet.

The date of its extinction is equally uncertain. Anthropologists have concluded from native legends (which may or may not refer to this monitor) that the *Megalania* was still alive less than a thousand years ago. But the remains actually found by naturalists look older than that.

The last item in this condensed list of missed opportunities
is that our naturalist should have been aboard the good ship
Heemskirk when its captain, Abel Janszoon Tasman, saw high
mountains rise from the sea on December 16, 1642. This
date marks the discovery of New Zealand. The modern naturalist would have made Tasman land instead of just sailing
on. He then would certainly have been able to show Tasman
a few moas.

Like the *Aepyornis* of Madagascar, the moas were ostrichlike birds, many of them very large. But there were also
smaller varieties. They were distributed over the three islands
which comprise New Zealand, the two large ones which are
now called North Island and South Island, and small Stewart
Island to the south of South Island. The qualifying statement "now called" was necessary because on some old maps
you can find the present Stewart Island labeled as South
Island. On these maps, the present South Island logically
appears under the name of Middle Island.

We know the moas mostly from their bones that have been
found in all three islands. In addition to the bones, a few
feathers are known and quite a large number of eggshells
that could be restored. Naturally we cannot tell which eggs
belonged to which bird, for comparative size is no guide. The
still living New Zealand kiwi, though probably not a direct
relative of the moas, is at least of the same general type, and
it throws any guesswork into the wastepaper basket. The
kiwi, a smallish bird, lays an egg which is far larger, by comparison, than that of the African ostrich. On the other hand,
the eggs of the cassowary are smaller than one would expect.

Footprints are known, too, of both the larger and the
smaller species. The small ones show a stride of not quite 20
inches, while the large ones show a stride of over 30 inches.
The large ones look surprisingly like some dinosaur footprints
of much greater age. In the case of the footprints as well as
of the length of the stride, there is a definite correlation be-

tween size of print and length of stride and the size of the bird. For this reason, at least some of the footprints can be tentatively ascribed to a species.

The moas of the past are now subdivided into five different genera, each with several species. It should be said at the outset that some of the species are doubtful, since they are based on only a few remains. It is quite possible that we have a few more species in our catalogues than existed in reality; it has happened with other extinct animals that male and female were classified as two different species if they differed considerably. However, the following is the tentative list of the moas, by genera:

Dinornis. The moas belonging to this genus were the tallest of the lot, their heads towering more than 12 feet above the ground. Largest of the six species was *Dinornis maximus.* All species were rather light-boned.

Euryapteryx. The moas of this genus were squat and heavy but not very tall, their heads being five to six feet above the ground. They must have been very numerous at certain times. There are five recognized species; a sixth is uncertain.

Megalapteryx. Two species from the South Island only. These were large for birds but small for moas, being not much over three feet tall. As the name of the genus indicates (from Greek *megas*, meaning large, and *apteryx*, the scientific name of the kiwi), they might also be taken for giant kiwis.

Emeus. Three recognized species with a fourth one uncertain, standing about four feet tall.

Anomalapteryx. Five species, most of them very early and rather small, of about the size of the *Megalapteryx* moas. One of these five species grew seven feet tall; it is also the most recent of this genus.

This list of genera, comprising just short of two dozen species, must not be misunderstood. At no time could one have found all twenty-two species alive on the islands. The best one could have expected would have been ten or eleven species alive simultaneously. Unfortunately, we cannot say what time that would have been. The era of the Homeric heroes—1000 B.C.—seems like a good guess.

By now, I have told what is really known about the moas; everything else is either unknown, or uncertain, or at least disputed.

Even the story of how the moas became known to science is rather complicated. The first explorer to land on New Zealand and to talk to the Maori living there was Captain James Cook, during his visit in November 1769. With the aid of interpreters who seem to have been of doubtful value, Captain Cook spoke to the Maori chieftain Tawaihura and asked him, among other things, about the animals occurring on the island.

Chief Tawaihura told the captain about a large and dangerous lizard—which must have been purely mythological, since no really large lizard does or did exist on New Zealand— but did not say a word about large birds. We can be rather certain now that there were no moas in the area where Tawaihura lived, even though they may still have existed elsewhere. With great fire and lack of logic, some scientists have made much of this omission, taking the negative evidence of Captain Cook's journals as positive proof that the moas became extinct at a much earlier date.

Beginning about the year 1800, people began to visit New Zealand and write books about their travels. Strangely enough, none of the first six books written on New Zealand (or about New Zealand) even mentions the moas. The first book to mention them does not use the name; it is a narrative that was published in London in 1838. Its writer was a trader by the name of Joel S. Polack and it is merely one more kink in the story that a missionary who knew Polack swore that Polack could not write.

Well, the book with Polack's name on it exists; the New York Public Library at Fifth Avenue and 42nd Street has a copy of it and I have read it myself. I cannot imagine that a trader can pursue his business and presumably make a profit without being able to write, but it might easily be that trader Polack did not write English and that the printed book is a translation of a manuscript in another language. At any event, trader Polack relates that he was shown very large bones and adds that the animals these bones came from were alive on the South Island. But he did not make clear what made him say so. Did the Maori tell him? Or did he draw this conclusion himself?

At about the time trader Polack was there, a Reverend William Colenso began hearing stories about gigantic birds from natives, and another missionary, the Reverend William Williams, started collecting moa bones.

The first moa relic to be placed into scientific hands was a large leg bone with both ends broken off. The year was 1839 and the hands which received this bone were very competent indeed, belonging to Professor Richard Owen, of London. They also happened to be reluctant hands—Professor Owen actually took it to be a soup bone at first glance. Even the simple fact that Owen received this bone has been embroidered nearly out of recognition. A story has it that "an illiterate sailor" left the bone for Owen when the professor was not at home.

Well, the man who took it there, and Owen was at home, was a sailor all right, but far from illiterate. He was the surgeon Dr. John Rule who had specifically traveled to England with the bone to see Professor Owen. When Owen was unimpressed, Rule persuaded him to devote more time to it.

Owen first "tried" the bone in the museum by holding it against the skeleton of a cow. It did not "fit." Owen tried the skeleton of a horse next. Finally, having run out of large mammals, he held it next to the leg of an ostrich skeleton. This was it! The bone matched that of the ostrich, except for size.

Once Owen was convinced, nothing could hold him back.

His colleagues, though admitting that it seemed to belong to a bird, suggested that he wait until more and undamaged bones became available. But Owen would have none of it. He knew that this was a bird bone, having belonged to a bird of the general build of an ostrich, but bigger and more massive by far. And since the bone was not fossil, the bird could not be dead for very long.

Thus Owen prepared a scientific report. It could not be very long, but what there was of it was very positive. Moreover, Owen reasoned, a layman does not know what to look for unless a scientist tells him. So he ordered the printing of 500 extra copies of his short report, to be distributed in New Zealand among missionaries, shipping agents and settlers. The 500 copies were crated for shipment to New Zealand to serve as a call for more evidence. But before the crate with the pamphlets had even crossed the equator, another crate arrived in London. It was full of moa bones, the bones collected by the Reverend Williams.

There was, it is reported, some ludicrous trouble with the Royal customs inspectors who found some kind of rule against the importing of bones. Fighting, so to speak, the British Museum and the Royal Society, not to mention Owen himself, the ones who lost were the customs inspectors. The final outcome of it all was a magnificent report by Professor Richard Owen.

A few years later, an interesting story came from New Zealand. Governor FitzRoy had met an old Maori chieftain by the name of Haumatangi. The year was 1844 and Haumatangi was about 85 years old. The old man told the governor proudly that he remembered seeing Captain Cook. Since the visit referred to was the one of November 1773, Haumatangi must have been about 14 at the time, so the claim sounded credible. Haumatangi added that the last moa in his province had been seen two years before Captain Cook's visit. This statement, of course, had to be taken on face value.

Another story which was circulated a little later had it that another chieftain, Kawana Paipai, said he had taken part in a moa hunt when he was a boy. The date figured out to be 1798 or 1799. Two or three other Maori, questioned around the middle of the last century about moas, declared that their grandfathers had told them about moa hunts. These dates all worked out to about 1770. It looked, therefore, as if the last moas were hunted to death around 1800.

In New Zealand itself, scientific opinions began to be sharply divided, the battle cry being, strangely enough, "the men of The Fleet" who did, or did not, find islands populated with moas. It has to be explained here that the Maori had come from islands near Tahiti in several waves of immigration. The main (and latest) wave is called The Fleet and the generally accepted date is "around 1350 A.D."

One school of thought—which became the minority party —had it that the Maori of The Fleet began to kill the moas for food and that the process of extermination was complete in Captain Cook's time. Another school of thought, however, claimed that the men of The Fleet arrived just about in time to see the last of the moas die.

It has to be said that everything written and printed about the moas in New Zealand for several decades was not written to establish facts, but to defend either the one or the other school of thought.

The ones who said the moas had died out very early had quite a number of ingenious arguments.

So-and-so-many Maori (say during the period from 1840 to 1860) did not know that moa bones had belonged to birds when they were shown them.

The word "moa" itself was used to mean "stone" or a raised small piece of land, like a flower bed.

There were only a very few proverbs and sayings in which the moas figured; they were usually figures of speech like "gone like the moa." These proverbs seemed to be centuries old.

As regards the statement that "my grandfather said that he hunted moas," it was pointed out that the words "grandfather" and "ancestor" are the same in the Maori language. As for old Haumatangi, he had probably just embellished on his memories of long ago hearing folk legends.

And Kawana Paipai was disposed of in two ways. One was that he also told about battles which were obviously invented. The other was that he had never made his statement about the moa hunt; the point being that there were at least three white witnesses to the statement and only one of them repeated it later.

In the meantime, places where moas had been slaughtered and cooked were found. There could be absolutely no doubt that humans and moas had lived together at one time. The problem was to say when.

Some scientists assumed a different native population, not only pre-Fleet but pre-Maori, which must have been the moa hunters. Other scientists said that the moa-hunter period did not have to be any other culture than Maori; they had been Maori of an earlier cultural level. This idea was contradicted mostly by the Maori themselves, who refused to believe that their ancestors should ever have changed, and who imagined the sailors of The Fleet to have been precisely like their fathers and grandfathers of about 1800. This, of course, just wasn't so—the Maori, like all peoples, changed considerably through the centuries.

Actually, everybody seems to be right depending on where you look. A number of moa-hunter campsites are indubitably Maori. Some others are almost certainly not Maori—of any cultural level. There seem to have been earlier castaways who settled on New Zealand and who did not come as organized immigrants like the Maori of The Fleet.

A fairly new scientific tool has been brought into play with some hopes of deciding the endless battle about the time of the moa hunters and, if possible, of the last of the moas. This tool is radio-carbon dating, or the C-14 method, which can tell the age of many things by their amount of carbon-14.

There are just two requirements. The first is that whatever it is that must be dated must once have been alive, bone or wood or even charcoal, for non-living things do not take up carbon-14 from the atmosphere. The second is that the object must not be older than 25,000 years or thereabouts; after that time, the carbon-14 is gone and the age becomes uncertain, except that it clearly is more than 25,000 years. Another aspect of the C-14 method is, unfortunately, that the object to be dated is destroyed in the process, so that scientists are rather handicapped when it comes to valuable specimens.

One *Dinornis* specimen was found in a freshwater deposit with its crop reasonably intact. And the crop was still full of food (plants) which could be sacrificed for dating. The result—these plants were eaten by the bird about 670 years ago or about 1300 A.D. To some, this was a surprisingly late date for *Dinornis*, because they had assumed that even the pre-Fleet Maori only knew the heavy *Euryapteryx* type.

The argument of whether the moa hunters were pre-Maori people, pre-Fleet Maori or just Maori after The Fleet must not be taken to mean that the extinction of the moas is placed squarely on the shoulders of the moa hunters, whoever they were.

Even if nobody had ever come to New Zealand prior to Captain Cook, the moas would probably be rare birds by now. They were completely flightless, they probably bred slowly, and they were most exceptionally stupid, for the brain of a six-foot moa was the same size as that of a turkey. Many moas died in swamps, indicating they probably could not swim. On the North Island, many perished at one time because of forest fires set by volcanic eruptions. There is some evidence of disease among the moas. But the main reason their numbers declined seems to have been a fairly small climatic change which diminished the open plains and increased the forest and swamp areas.

The moas were obviously on the downgrade for natural reasons. The moa hunters merely helped along and may have provided the final touch in the demise of the moa. But when was that?

Nobody will commit himself.

The proof that even the tall *Dinornis* type was still active and alive at the time of The Fleet has been rather a blow to some of the archeologists of New Zealand. In the course of time, the party which had proclaimed a very early date for the last of the moas had succeeded in attaining the position of "the voice of science." What they said was "science" and what the others had said was either amateurish, or just the spirit of the nineteenth century, or else a wrong conclusion due to lack of evidence that has become known since—the phrasing depended to some extent on whose opinion was being demolished.

In one point, however, even the most conservative wing of the New Zealand scientists was rather lenient. It was admitted that small moas of the *Megalapteryx* type may have survived until quite recent times on the South Island. Roger Duff, the Director of the Canterbury Museum in New Zealand (and one of those "shocked" by the outcome of the carbon-14 dating), dates two Maori-made artifacts using moa skin and moa feathers as from the seventeenth and eighteenth centuries respectively. Roger Duff's dating, incidentally, is based entirely on archeological and ethnological evidence.

Zoologists seem to feel that something must be wrong, even though they can't say what or why.

The simple fact is that some of the moa remains do not look as old as the archeologists say they must be. And New

Zealand is not a place with a dry climate which tends to preserve animal remains indefinitely.

It is interesting that the most recent story of a moa hunt came from the South Island, in fact from the southwestern end of the South Island where the *Takahe*—scientific name *Notornis*—was finally discovered alive after having been thought extinct.

That story takes up just one part of one paragraph in Vol. II of Sir Walter Lawry Buller's *History of the Birds of New Zealand,* published in London in 1888. The sentence reads: "Sir George Grey tells me that in 1868 he was at Preservation Inlet and saw a party of natives there who gave him a circumstantial account of the recent killing of a small Moa, describing with much spirit its capture out of a drove of six or seven."

That's all, but it might be prudent to say that Sir George Grey had been, in succession, governor of South Australia, twice governor of New Zealand and then governor of the Cape Colony—in short, not somebody you would expect to make up tales.

It is true that there has been no report since then, at least not one that could be called definite. But there still *are* virtually unknown areas on the South Island. Maybe the last of the moas, even if a small type, is still somewhere around. I don't assert that this must be the case. But there is also no reason for stating categorically that the final chapter has been written.

11

Let's Build an Extraterrestrial!

FOR AT LEAST the last three decades, a large number of science fiction writers have been confronted, at one time or another, with the problem of constructing extraterrestrial life-forms. Naturally the professional chemists and biologists who write science fiction on the side did best, not so much because their professional knowledge led them for long distances on hitherto untrodden paths, but because it made them stop at the right moment.

As regards those who were primarily writers, the results make one suspect that they at first tried to apply what biology they knew. Since this apparently did not get them very far, they presumably threw overboard whatever it was they had not quite arrived at and wrote things like this: "Surprisingly, the aliens were quite human in shape, the only major differences, or at any event the ones which were easily visible, being a strong tail and a bluish complexion."

Or else, if the actual contact with the aliens could be fleeting, they resorted to saying that the forms the Earthmen beheld were so alien, so outside of all terrestrial experience, that it was impossible to describe them.

All this refers to recent science fiction, of course. Now let's take a quick look back to the forerunners of modern science fiction and see whether they did any better.

The first man who seriously attempted to think up life-forms of another heavenly body (the Moon, in this case) was the great Johannes Kepler, when wrestling with his book *Somnium*, which he never really finished. The planetary conditions he had in mind consisted of a rocky surface with many caves, large and small, and broiling sunshine through a thin atmosphere. Hence the creatures of the Moon mostly have the shape of terrestrial snakes, to be able to escape the deadly sunshine quickly and thoroughly.

Of the science fiction writers of the nineteenth century, I am selecting three and naturally the list has to be headed by Jules Verne. I think that I have read all of Verne and, unless a minor work escaped me, I can only report that he refrained from building any extraterrestrials whatever.

Jules Verne's compatriot and contemporary Achille Eyraud (in his *Voyage à Vénus*) and his English contemporary Percy Greg (in his novel about a trip to Mars *Across the Zodiac*) were both proficient in describing pretty girls, but the only alien creature I remember is a flying snake in Greg's book.

As for Sydney Whiting's *Heliondé: or, Adventures in the Sun*, published in London in 1855, which is based on Sir William Herschel's notion that the Sun is a dark body with a luminous atmosphere, it can hardly be considered science fiction. But even if it is, it does not offer much in the line of extraterrestrial creatures; a fairly typical example of the things you encounter is a bush which does not grow seed pods but cakes of perfumed soap.

Unlike Jules Verne, H. G. Wells went in quite heavily for extraterrestrials in his earlier years. When the engineer Cavor goes to the Moon, he finds gigantic moon calves and a ruling race modeled both in bodily and in social organization after the ants or termites of Earth. I think that Wells is the original inventor of the giant insects which have plagued science fiction editors ever since. But, as you also know, when Wells' Martians come to Earth, they turn out to be air-breathing octopi in shape—not, as has been said on many occasions, a very likely shape.

However, the occasional science fiction writer of the past was not the only type of creative genius who did, or could have, exerted ingenuity in the building of an extraterrestrial. There were many others who engaged in a very similar line of endeavor for the purpose of representing gods, demons or just outlandish creatures, somewhat along the line of the Midnight Marvels to which I devoted a column some months ago.

To put it bluntly, nobody showed much imagination and the method was standardized at an early age:

Combine the features of various kinds of living creatures into something that could be drawn, painted or sculptured and the job was done. Put a woman's head on a feline body and you had a sphinx. Add the head of a bird to the body of a man and you had ibis-headed Thoth. Take a horse and supply it with the wings of an eagle and Pegasus was ready for flight, though with lateral stability only. Take another horse, cut off its head and graft the upper half of a man's body to it and the centaur was ready.

Christianity brushed away these particular examples, but the method must have remained, for at one point St. Bernard had harsh words to say about decorations he encountered in monasteries:

"What business have those ridiculous monstrosities, those amazingly freakish beauties and marvelously beautiful freaks in the cloisters right in front of the eyes of the monks who are supposed to be reading or meditating? You see one head with many bodies or one body with many heads. Here you have a serpent's tail attached to a quadruped and there a mammal's head attached to a fish's body. There you have a creature that is half horse and half goat and here one with horns and the rear end of a horse."

Just what business such creations had in a cloister is a still unanswered question, but artists just could not think of another method.

The fabulous unicorn was drawn as a horse with the feet of a goat and a narwhale's tusk on its forehead. The mermaid— a fairly late invention—was a woman from forehead to waist and a fish below that. (Virgil Partch, in a recent cartoon, put the left-over halves together as an alternate choice.) And

Fig. 32. Flying snake from Gesner.

the traditional picture of the devil was that of a man with two small goat's horns, one goat leg and a tail. Demons differed from devils by having a few more incongruous parts added to an improbable anatomy.

Fig. 33. The Forest Devil, said to have been caught in Switzerland.

Even when it came to something as simple, comparatively speaking, as the legendary Hydra, the extirpation of which was one of the feats of Hercules, the artists stuck to their formula. The story spoke of a seven-headed snake and this should not be a very hard task for an artist. What he did draw was the body of an exceedingly well-nourished snake with seven heads that might be described as humanized lion faces and with two, just two, lion paws with six toes.

We do not know who made this drawing; it was preserved for us by Konrad Gesner in his *Historia animalium* with a warning that his readers should not take the Hydra to have been historical reality. But the same book contained "flying snakes," since classical authors had vouchsafed their existence. Some just had wings. Others had wings and feet.

A far more complicated creature was the Forest Devil, also from Gesner, an unclassified and unclassifiable beast caught just once in a Swiss forest. Here the artist went all out: the body is that of a mammal with a tail, the legs are human but with bird feet, the arms human with lion's paws. The creature has a beard and the masculine article is used throughout in the description—but there are pronounced pendulous breasts.

And then you had the really complicated creatures, the griffin, the dragon and the basilisk. In the case of the basilisk, the legend was definite on a few things: the basilisk was the king of the serpents and came into being when a seven-year-old rooster laid an egg which was hatched either by a toad or by the Sun. In appearance, then, it had to have both characteristics, those of serpents and those of the rooster.

I offer two attempts to combine these characteristics.

The artist who drew the picture for Sebastian Munster's *Cosmographia* more or less settled for a lizard's body with a long tail. The head—wearing a crown—was mostly that of a rooster and there were eight rooster's feet, four on each side.

The other picture (artist also unknown) is from an old German natural history book. In this design, the rooster largely won out, except for the long reptilian tail and the wings, which are not bird wings. The griffin is a wild mixture of bird and mammal all the way through, while the dragon is, in this case, a comparatively tame creature. More often, it appeared as an enormous crocodile with gigantic bat wings.

That a random combination can do almost as well is illustrated by a game my wife used to play with our two daughters. In that game, one of the three participants would start by drawing a head, which could be either human or animal. Then the head was folded under, leaving only the lines of the neck visible, and the next player could go on from there, knowing only that it was a neck. And so forth.

In one particular case, resulting in a bug-eyed monster which could quite easily have graced (if that's the word) the cover of certain magazines at a certain period, the daughter who drew the head obviously had some sort of fairy tale caterpillar in mind. The mind of the next player was on cats, but the first still stuck to caterpillars. The one who had cats in mind produced the skirt of which the hem remained visible, so that the dancer's legs resulted.

So you obviously cannot produce a biologically possible or even believable creature by the (random or artistic) combination of separate parts. Fine—but how *can* you go about it? All I can say offhand is that it isn't easy; so much depends on so many different circumstances.

There is, in the first place, the planetary environment, consisting of such factors as either much water or very little water; temperature which depends mainly but not only on the distance of the planet from its sun; seasonal changes which depend on the inclination of the axis of rotation of a planet to the plane of its orbit around the sun.

Fig. 34. Top: *The basilisk, from Munster's* Cosmographia. Bottom: *The basilisk, hatched from a rooster's egg.*

It depends on the presence or absence of a large moon (or moons) because, with a large and nearby moon, you get pronounced tides, while without a moon, or only very small moons, you only have the solar tide, which is likely to be unimpressive.

The relative abundance of the chemical elements in the outer crust and in the atmosphere certainly also plays a role.

Let us, for a first test, take our two neighbors in the Solar System, Venus inside the Earth's orbit and Mars outside it.

When I started reading books on science, as a schoolboy, Venus, in most of them, was firmly declared to be a *panthalassa*, the technical term for a planet completely covered by water without any land showing. This, after various attempts to be "different," has recently been revived by Whipple and Menzel.

Now such a shoreless ocean—I am avoiding all other consideration and am concentrating on just the one fact that it is an ocean—can harbor virtually everything in abundance. But with limitations; you can't just mix the fauna of the equatorial Pacific Ocean of today with equatorial seas of the Jurassic and Cretaceous periods and obtain a believable or even possible picture.

You can have, if you want to, most of the arthropods, lobsters and sea spiders, trilobites and, if you insist, something like a sea-going centipede. But you must specify that there are shallow areas in this ocean if you want to have clams, for they don't grow too far down. You can have jellyfish in fantastic numbers of species as well as individuals.

You can have octopi and all sorts of fishes. But you can't have a turtle, for example, because when, in Earth's past, some fishes went up on land, they first produced what we now call amphibia—say, primitive salamanders—and the reptiles, the birds and the mammals came afterward. They all are creatures of the land, even though some reptiles, like the turtles and the sea snakes, and some mammals, like the whales and the seals, returned to the ocean at a later date.

And don't make anything more intelligent than the most intelligent fish—I don't know which fish that is or could be —for the open sea is a region of steady movement and no intelligence is needed for that. The exceptions to the statement that this is a region of movement are armored forms like clams, but a perfectly sessile creature which relies on its armor for individual protection and on numerous offspring for survival of the species also is not going to develop intelligence. It doesn't need any.

So a shoreless Venusian ocean—I repeat I am concentrating on no other fact than that it is a shoreless ocean—might harbor a very varied life and some forms may be rather pretty. But I challenge anybody to think up an aquatic form of life, especially among the invertebrates, which would look radically different from what we have in our oceans. The multitude of forms on our own planet is so overwhelming that one always gets the impression that anything that can survive with the shape it has is also in existence.

One thing is absolutely needed in this shoreless ocean if it is to have any life at all. There must be plants, microscopic or otherwise, because animal life alone is an impossibility.

You know the old tall tale about the man who made a living by having a mouse and cat farm. The cats, of course, ate the mice, and when the cats were big enough, he killed and skinned them, sold the pelts and fed the cat's bodies to the mice. Even if the mice were carnivorous, this just wouldn't work. Somewhere at the beginning of such a cycle, there has to be the original food producer, the plant, which makes living (and edible, as a rule) tissue out of dissolved minerals, carbon dioxide and sunlight for energy.

I might as well, at this point, present two strong hints at caution. If, in that sea, you have a tribe of *Kraken*, octopi a mile in circumference and the largest thing in the ocean, don't make them smart. If they are the largest thing in the ocean, immune to all danger except an occasional outburst of the elements, such as a submarine volcano opening up, and, of course, old age, they don't have to be intelligent. What has been said about oysters a while ago applies also to the invulnerable life-form.

Likewise, don't make something one millimeter in diameter into an intelligent life-form. Some time ago, somebody wrote a story in which the main character, who was not a hero, caught what he thought to be a shiny wasp. It stung him so hard that he had to let go—and then noticed to his surprise that the wasp sting made his Geiger counter chatter wildly. The implication was, of course, that this was a tiny spaceship with atomic drive.

Though I liked the story, I knew that this could never happen. In order to be intelligent enough to even discover atomic energy, a being has to have a rather large number of brain cells. These brain cells must be nourished, which needs organs for eating and digesting food. The digestive tract must be protected by some covering and this package must be moved around in some manner so that it can find food. It must also move around to avoid being eaten, at least until it has attained the intelligence that splits atoms and controls what they do after splitting.

It has been said and bolstered with many pounds of statistics that, in a modern army, 98 men are needed to enable two men to shoot at the enemy. This relationship must apply also to the number of cells needed to support the brain cells that do the thinking. Since a cell, in order to function as a cell, must consist of a very large number of molecules and since the size of molecules is a given fact, there must be a minimum size for a functioning cell.

L. Sprague de Camp, who was to my knowledge the first to present this chain of reasoning (in a two-part article in *Astounding*, May and June issues of 1939), came to the conclusion that an overall body weight of around 40 pounds would be needed if you want intelligence on the human level.

It is possible that a few facts permit a little more stretching, so that the minimum weight could be less. But the reasoning itself is valid and the reduction cannot be very much. Whether the first interstellar hero has to establish relations with something weighing 45 or only 30 pounds does not make much of a difference.

But I did not want to slip out of our solar system yet.

Now if we look at Mars, we are helped no end by the fact that we know a great deal about it. Here is a small planet with very little water and a thin atmosphere consisting mostly of inert nitrogen. It is generally a cold planet, but during the summer the equatorial regions can attain temperatures between 60 and 70 degrees Fahrenheit at noon. To make our problem still easier, we are virtually certain that we see plant life.

The dark greenish patches which all bear nice classical names due to Signor Schiaparelli of half a century ago cannot just be mineral discolorations. When covered up by yellow dust from the deserts, they manage to break through again and just during the last close approach of Mars, in 1954, Dr. Earl C. Slipher, working at Bloemfontein, South Africa, found a new one almost the size of Texas under about 15° northern Martian latitude and about 235° Martian longitude, which means about halfway between the northern end of *Syrtis major* and *Trivium Charontis*, two well-known Martian markings.

There has been a lot of discussion recently in learned journals on whether any terrestrial plant could grow on Mars, and if so, which one. Naturally any suggestion made by anybody was countered with heavy arguments by somebody else. But the fact remains that we see something growing on Mars which is, in our terminology, plant life. If we do not understand their biochemistry under the conditions we are forced to assume from astronomical observations, this can only mean one of two things:

Either we cannot observe all the conditions and something which we have missed, or are bound to miss with present instrumentation, is a perfectly fine explanation; or else we don't know enough biochemistry and there is a way of living and growing under these conditions.

The reasoning that forced us to say that there must be plant life in the Venusian oceans, if we want animal life of any kind, almost forces us to say that, since there are plants on Mars, there must be something that we would call animals.

Some biologists with whom I discussed this stated with professional caution that this reasoning does not necessarily hold true. I don't agree. Speaking in the largest sense, the animals of Earth, from sow bugs to elephants, are parasitic on plants. Now life, at least on Earth, behaves in such a manner that *if* there is something to be parasitic on, something else will be happy to take over the role of the parasite.

Something feeding on these Martian plants must have the power of movement because it needs so much plant tissue for its own sustenance that the rate of the plant growth cannot furnish the necessary amount. Hence it must be capable of locomotion.

Whether this supposed Martian plant-eater is built along the lines of a locust, or along the lines of a desert tortoise, or along those of a rabbit is something entirely different again. One can assume that it simply freezes into a death-like state during the cold Martian night and remains in that state until thawed out by the Sun. In that case, it could be insect-like in organization.

One can assume with equal justification that the "animal," at the first sign of cold in the evening, burrows into the ground for a few feet and goes to sleep normally in an environment where the temperature may be quite cold, but where there is very little deviation from whatever temperature it may have. In that case, it could be something comparable to a desert tortoise.

Or you can make the assumption that it has an internal mechanism like the birds and mammals of Earth, something producing heat. Then it does not have to dig itself in. All it needs is an effective heat insulator around its body, which might be hairlike, or featherlike, or, if this sounds more "alien," something like bark or sponge rubber.

So far, I have mostly talked about extraterrestrial animal life in order to show some of the difficulties. When it comes to an extraterrestrial *intelligent* life-form, the difficulties rapidly increase in number and kind.

It may come as a surprise, but the first tentative recipe for the construction of an intelligent extraterrestrial was written by the Dutch physicist, philosopher and astronomer Christian Huyghens. The title of the book is *Kosmotheoros* and it appeared posthumously, in 1692, at first in Latin. Nobody seems to know just when Huyghens wrote the major portion of the book.

He said there that an extraterrestrial must have eyes and ears—that is, senses "and pleasure arising from his senses." He must know the art of writing to remember things, arithmetic and geometry to understand relationships, hands to make things—and he must be upright.

It does not become quite clear from Huyghens' book why he must be upright. It sounds as if Huyghens made this condition to free the forelimbs from the task of locomotion so that there are "hands to make things."

The insistence struck me as amusing because Sprague de Camp, in the articles mentioned, also was insistent on that point, but more for mechanical reasons. The brain must be protected against shock as much as possible and the more bone, cartilage and tissue there is between the feet, which take the shocks, and the brain, the better.

All this is sound logic and it is obvious that the body of the extraterrestrial must be such that it functioned well as an animal body before it grew to be intelligent. Of course, one can postulate that accidental environmental conditions of the past helped along.

Around the turn of the century, a number of biologists and zoologists toyed with the idea that Man had evolved in what they called an asylum, an area accidentally free from large predatory animals and with a gentle climate. They obviously did not think much of the human body as a well-functioning animal. We now know that they were wrong and that the idea of the "asylum" is not needed. But it may conceivably have happened somewhere else, for the Galaxy must be full of planets and possibilities.

There is just one major difficulty in imagining a believable intelligent extraterrestrial—we have never seen one. What I mean by this remark is this:

We know the organization of living animal tissue on Earth. We know that the organization of the mammal is superior. True, it "wastes" food by making its own heat, but this fact makes it climatically independent. And though a reptile can do quite well in the proper climate, it is very limited. When the air grows too cold, it must be inactive, though it usually survives. When the air grows too hot, it dies of heat stroke, for, lacking a temperature-regulating mechanism, it not only cannot keep warm, it also cannot keep cool.

Now this vertebrate body, whether mammalian or reptilian, has *two* pairs of limbs and usually a tail. What we don't know is whether it *has* to be built that way.

To use a classical example: we don't know whether the centaur shape is possible or not. On Earth, it doesn't exist; that much is certain. But is this due to an anatomical necessity for which we don't know the reason or did it just happen that way here?

As for comparatively minor matters, we do know that they just happened. Genus Homo is tailless and almost hairless. But it doesn't *have* to be hairless and tailless to invent writing, to build and ride cars and to engage in research, politics and crime.

If we had fur and a tail, our fashions, habits and morals would be different, but if brain and senses and hands were unchanged, we'd still write books and symphonies, build houses, ships and airplanes—and try to build an extraterrestrial.

12

The Laws of Utter Chaos

TELEGRAPH, TELEPHONE, RADIO, KODAK AND TELSTAR have it in common that they are coined words, invented for the purpose of naming something that did not exist before, and most people know that they are coined words.

But few are aware that the word "gas" is a coined word too, which differs from the others mainly in being much older, about three hundred and fifty years by now. No precise figure can be given because it is not known when it was coined. But we do know who coined it, namely the Flemish physician and experimenter Jan Baptista van Helmont. He was born in Brussels, probably in 1577 and died at Vilvoorde, not far from his birthplace, probably in 1644.

If Jan Baptista van Helmont had lived a century or two later, he would have been a greater scientist than he managed to be in his time. Van Helmont was a man of original ideas who made experiments never before performed, but he was handicapped by the general lack of chemical and physical knowledge of his time. One of van Helmont's original experiments—he is half-jokingly referred to as the "father of hydroponics" because of it—was to plant a small willow tree in a soil-filled tub. The soil had been carefully weighed before it was placed in the tub and nothing was ever added to it but plain water. Five years later the tree had gained 164 pounds but the soil had lost only two ounces—at least that is how van Helmont's figures translate into our system. A van

Helmont of 1740 or 1840 would then have started an investigation into what the plant had "eaten" during those five years; the actual van Helmont concluded that the water had "hardened" into wood and leaves and quickly retrogressed to early Greek philosophical speculation.

But the tree-growing experiment was a side-issue. One of the investigations carried out by van Helmont dealt with a gas formed when wood was burned (our CO_2) and he came to the conclusion that this was something different from air, though similar in many respects. Since the normal vocabulary had words only for solid and liquid substances but lacked a word for substances like air, he coined the word "gas", from the Greek *chaos* the original meaning of which is "unformed".

At first the word gas was meant to be used for gases other than air (which, of course, was assumed to be homogeneous) but soon air was included. Unfortunately at a later date, say from 1750 until well into the nineteenth century, English-writing authors fell into the habit of writing "air" where we would say "gas". Joseph Black called carbon dioxide "fixed air", Henry Cavendish called hydrogen "flammable air" and others referred to nitrogen as "dephlogisticated air". Van Helmont's accomplishment was all but forgotten for a while.

His works were published after his death (in 1644) under the overall title *Ortus medicinae* (The Garden of Health) since he considered himself mainly a physician. But he has to be mentioned first when it comes to the exploration of the physical behavior of gases, for he gave them their name.

The second man to be considered was a botanist, though only later in his life. Born in Scotland on December 21, 1773 the boy was baptized by his father (an Anglican parson) Robert Brown, and in time Robert Brown began to study medicine. He then joined the army as a medical officer but gradually drifted into botany which was then closely allied to medicine.

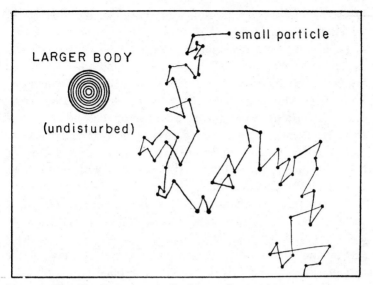

small particle

LARGER BODY

(undisturbed)

Fig. 35. *The "Brownian motion" of a small particle in water, as seen under a microscope.*

As a botanist he became famous for discovering that every plant cell has a nucleus. In fact he invented the term, using the diminutive of *nuca*, the Latin word for "nut". But much of his fame rests on another discovery, one that has absolutely nothing to do with botany, though Robert Brown thought at first that it did.

One day in 1827 he looked at pollen floating in water. With the aid of his microscope, which he probably used because he intended to identify the pollen by their size and shape, he saw that they were in steady motion. It was an irregular motion, not leading anywhere, but they would not hold still for a moment. The fact that pollen behaved like this when immersed in water was new and Brown looked for an explanation. It occurred to him quickly.

Pollen grains, after all, were not dead matter. Fern or other plants would sprout from them in time. Since they were alive, the steady zig-zagging motion was caused by the "life force" which they harbored.

To us this is no explanation at all but an expression of a mistaken belief, but in 1827 it could still be advanced. It so happened that Brown, at a later date, observed the same kind of motion on particles of dye suspended in water. These particles certainly were not alive and never had been. Robert Brown dutifully reported his discovery in a scientific journal and admitted that he could not explain it. It is an interesting sidelight that Albert Einstein still wrestled with the mathematics of the explanation.

Actually the explanation for the "Brownian motion", as it came to be called was already in existence at the time the discovery was made. Brown either did not know about it, or else did not believe it. It is also possible that he knew of the explanation but did not think that it applied to his observation. That explanation was the atomic theory of John Dalton, first announced in 1803 and published with much detail in 1808.

Dalton's idea that all matter had to consist of atoms was an outgrowth of the belief held by Robert Boyle and Sir Isaac Newton that gases had to consist of discrete particles. And both Boyle and Newton had been impressed by work done by the Italian Evangelista Torricelli. Since Torricelli lived from 1608 to 1645, this brings us right back to the time of van Helmont, when most of the fundamental discoveries still had to be made.

Evangelista Torricelli was thirty years of age when he read the works of Galileo Galilei. Needless to say that he was much impressed, as was everybody who actually read Galilei's works, instead of just picking out a few sentences for the purpose of disputing them. Four years later he went to the Villa Arcetri (near Florence) where Galileo Galilei was "imprisoned" and stayed on as secretary and companion to the old and blind man. Galilei died three months later. But during that time there had been a discussion between the two that led to the work that made Torricelli famous.

Galilei still believed in the *horror vacui*, as it was then called, the notion that "Nature abhors a vacuum". There was "proof" for this. If you dipped a tube into water and then pulled a piston up the tube, the water rose in the tube. It could not stay behind, because in doing so a vacuum would have been created and since Nature did not permit a vacuum to exist, the water had to follow the piston.

But ordinary engineering experience, accumulated while building tall buildings, said that water could not be raised by more than 33 feet in this manner. Galileo Galilei suggested that Torricelli look into this problem.

Torricelli did and began to reason. Powerful winds could topple trees, hence air could exert a pressure. Wind pressure was a lateral phenomenon, but maybe air *always* exerted pressure downward. If so the pressure might only be enough to push water to a height of 33 feet, but not more.

That happens to be inconveniently large for easy experimentation; but there was a much heavier liquid known, namely mercury. Torricelli filled a bowl with mercury and then filled a glass tube, closed at one end, with the same metal. Then he turned the glass tube upside down and into the bowl of mercury. Some of the mercury promptly flowed from the tube into the bowl, but not very much. A column of mercury, 30 inches tall, remained in the glass tube.

Evidently air pressure was equivalent to the weight of 30 inches of mercury and the empty space above the mercury in the tube had to be that impossibility: a vacuum.

It is called a Torricellian vacuum to this day, even though it is not a very good vacuum because it contains mercury vapor.

This simple experiment produced a scientific revolution. If the air could exert only so much pressure it meant that it had only so much weight. This, in turn, meant that the at-

mosphere had to have only a certain height—and the concept
of the air ocean was born. Blaise Pascal in France began to
think about it and reasoned that, if that were true, the air
pressure on top of a high mountain should be less than the
air pressure in the lowlands. Pascal lived in the Auvergne and
there was a mountain handy: the Puy-de-Dome. Since he was
chronically sick the idea of climbing a mountain did not ap-
peal to him—though the exercise might have done him a lot
of good—and he charged his younger brother-in-law, one
Monsieur Perier, with the task of carrying a Torricellian tube
to the peak of the mountain. This was done in 1646 and it
was found that the air pressure on top of the Puy-de-Dome
(its height is 4790 feet) was actually less by about six inches
than at its foot. Knowing this one could try to calculate the
depth of the air ocean, or the height of the atmosphere and
it was Dr. Edmond Halley in England who was one of the
first to try to do so, proclaiming a three-layered atmosphere
with a total height of 45 miles.

One man who was much intrigued by these findings was
Otto von Guericke (1602-1686), Burgomaster of the city of
Magdeburg. Intent on producing a vacuum he invented an
air pump and in 1654, in Regensburg, he gave the spectacu-
lar demonstration consisting of two teams of horses trying to
pull apart a metallic sphere, consisting of two hemispheres,
from which the air had been evacuated. Otto von Guericke
carefully studied air pressure and when, on December 5, 1660
he found that the air pressure was unusually low he predicted a storm—which promptly happened the following day.

Robert Boyle, born in December 1627 at Lismore Castle,
Ireland, was one of the many children of the Earl of Cork. He
was just thirty years old when he heard of von Guericke's air
pump. He and his assistant, a then twenty-two year old young
man by the name of Robert Hooke, who later became Secretary of the Royal Society, tried to build a pump like von
Guericke's and ended up with a better one.

Boyle knew, of course, that air can be compressed and he was interested in the relationship between volume and pressure. To find out he built a kind of adaptation of Torricelli's tube, a tube in which gas could be compressed by the weight of mercury. If he started out with a given volume of air and then doubled the amount of mercury the air was compressed to half its original volume.

As he put it in an appendix to his original publication (1662):

> "It is evident, that as common air, when reduced to half its wonted extent, obtained near about twice as forcible a spring as it had before; so this thus comprest air being further thrust into this narrow room, obtained thereby a spring about as strong again as that it last had, and consequently four times as strong as that of the common air. And their is no cause to doubt, that if we had been here furnished with a greater quantity of quick-silver and a very strong tube, we might, by a further compression of the included air, have made it counterbalance the pressure of a far taller and heavier cylinder of mercury."

What later became known as "Boyle's law" was simply the fact that tripling the pressure reduced the volume to one third, quadrupling it reduced the volume to one quarter and so forth. Boyle drew the logical conclusion: the air must consist of discrete particles with a vacuum between them. If you exerted pressure you forced the particles to be closer to each other.

With all his experiments about the "spring" of compressed air, Boyle lost sight of his original idea, namely to see whether a mercury column more than 30 inches in height would be counterbalanced. And he never gave a single thought to temperature. It was the French physicist Edme Mariotte who realized that Boyle's law held strictly true only if the temperature of the air did not change. Mariotte had learned that a volume of air expanded if the temperature increased and

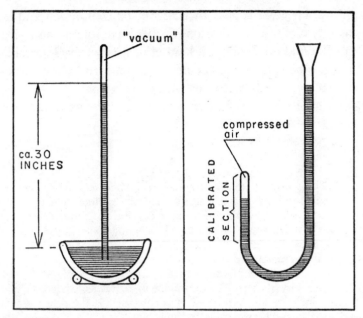

Fig. 36. Two mercury-filled glass tubes that shook the scientific world. At left Torricelli's tube, the later barometer, at right Robert Boyle's tube for compressing air.

shrank if the temperature decreased—a discovery which finally led to the production of liquefied gases with all their numerous applications. As may be expected, Boyle's law, in French textbooks, is "Mariotte's law", and I am voting on the side of the French.

By the year 1700, then, it had been established that air had weight, that a vacuum was possible, that air could be artificially compressed into a smaller space and, finally, that it expanded when heated and contracted when cooled and that all that only made sense if one assumed that it consisted of separate particles. A solid, like lead, or a liquid, like water, did not seem to consist of separate particles since they could not be compressed. For a while, even after Mariotte, nobody noticed that a red-hot iron bar had a larger volume than a cold one.

The next chapter in the history of the gases is purely chemical. Jan Baptista van Helmont had discovered carbon dioxide, a gas other than air. Hydrogen was the next gas to be discovered. That there is a "flammable air" is first mentioned in the works of a Frenchman named Turquet de Mayerne—in the posthumous edition of his work, published in 1702. But the early investigator of hydrogen—though he cannot be called its discoverer—was Henry Cavendish. He was born in Nice on the Riviera in 1731 because his mother, Lady Anne Cavendish, had gone there for her health. Henry Cavendish

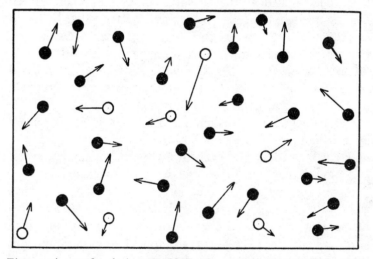

Fig. 37. *A sample of air, magnified a few trillion times. Black stands for nitrogen, open circles for oxygen, arrows indicate direction of motion and (by their length) the velocity of motion.*

attended Cambridge University, but without obtaining a degree; he was interested in knowledge, not in degrees or titles. He also was a very strange man in all his habits. He could speak to only one person at a time and that only when that

person was known to him and was male. Later in life he refused even to be in the same room with a woman and gave
his instructions to his maids in writing. To round out the
picture he acquired two enormous inheritances from older
relatives when he was himself over fifty; the fortunes were so
large that the French physicist Jean Baptiste Biot called him:
*le plus riche de tous les savants et le plus savant de tous les
riches*, which can be (inadequately) translated as: "the
richest of all the savants and the most knowledgeable of all
the rich". And since he used far less than the interest on his
fortune, he died being the largest depositor in the Bank of
England.

Cavendish died at the age of seventy-nine—when he felt
death approaching he sent his servants away so that he might
die alone—and left a scientific legacy of work accomplished
in astronomy, meteorology, metallurgy and a few other fields,
but mainly chemistry. As for hydrogen, he had obtained it
from metals by the action of acids, had carefully collected it
over mercury and named it "flammable air from metals". He
not only knew that it was flammable, he knew that it was far
lighter than air—thereby establishing that different gases had
different densities. He burned hydrogen, producing water
and proved that way that water was not an element.

It was already known that air consisted of at least two
gases, nitrogen (discovered in 1772 by the Scottish physician
Daniel Rutherford) and oxygen (discovered by Antoine Lau-
rent Lavoisier in 1774 or 1775), and Cavendish found out
that these two gases, merely mixed normally, could be forced
into a chemical compound by the passage of electric sparks.

But no matter how much oxygen he added to a sample of
nitrogen, there always remained a bubble that would not
combine. It was argon. Cavendish missed an important discovery by a hair.

These discoveries, plus a few others (like the one by the
French chemist Joseph Louis Proust—1754-1826—that each

chemical compound contains its elements in definite propor-
tions) paved the way for John Dalton, who arrived at the
conclusion that *all* matter, and not just gases, had to consist
of atoms. Of course it was thought at first that only two atoms would get together for the simpler compounds. The
"fixed air" of Joseph Black was thought to have the formula
CO (instead of CO_2), and water was believed to be HO (instead of H_2O). But even so it was impractical to talk about
an "atom" of water, or a "compound atom" as some phrased
it. It was Count Amadeo Avogadro (1776-1856) who coined
the term molecule, the meaning being "small bundle". He
also suggested that even the elements came in molecules, con-
taining more than one atom as a rule.

Strangely enough the atomic theory of Dalton, which con-
stituted a scientific revolution, was accepted quietly—while
Avogadro's idea of molecules, which was merely a refinement,
caused violent opposition.

After this interlude, during which gases were treated
mainly as chemicals, physics began to reassert itself. The
turning point was around the middle of the nineteenth century.

An important point was that both Avogadro and Andre
Marie Ampere (1775-1836) had independently arrived at the
conclusion that a given volume of a gas, at a given temperature, would contain the same number of atoms (molecules)
regardless of the nature of the gas. Naturally, that brought
up the question: how many?

Again we have to backtrack.

Jacques Alexandre Cesar Charles (1746-1823), the inventor of the hydrogen-filled balloon, had discovered in 1787
that gases shrank at a definite rate when cooled. For each
degree centigrade of heat they lost, they also lost one 273
part of the volume. If this rule held true all the way, they
should have no volume at all at a temperature of *minus 273°*
centigrade. A long time later, in 1848, Lord Kelvin (born Wil-

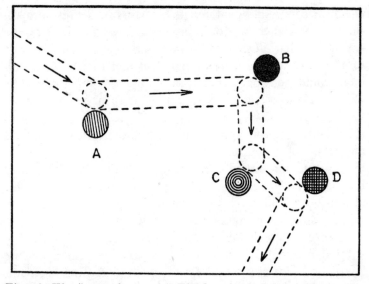

Fig. 38. The "mean free path." The length of the path traveled between collisions is never the same twice running, but it averages out to the theoretical mean free path.

liam Thompson, 1824-1907) went back to this discovery, suggesting that at *minus* 273° centigrade the gas might have lost all of its energy, not its volume, and that this temperature should be used as a starting point for a temperature scale that avoided the nuisance of "below zero" degrees.

From then on things moved fast. In 1857 the German physicist Rudolph Clausius (1822-1888) invented a new concept. A gas, he said, consists of "atoms" in steady motion, flying in all directions. Hence they must collide quite often. But while the distance between collisions would not be the same, there should be an average distance between collisions, that average distance depending on both density and temperature. This average distance is now known in English as the "mean free path". In 1860 the Scottish mathematician James Clark Maxwell (1831-1879) began to think about these problems.

Maxwell felt that even for a given temperature the speed of the molecules would not be uniform. Some would move faster than the norm, and others more slowly; and it was only the *average* of these different velocities that corresponded to the temperature. Raise the temperature and you get a higher average molecular velocity, but a specific molecule might move at a rate corresponding to a temperature twenty degrees lower. While Maxwell, sitting in Cambridge, pursued these thoughts, Ludwig Boltzmann (1884-1906), professor at the University of Vienna, conceived the same idea. Consequently the kinetic theory of gases that emerged from their separate goosequills was later referred to as the Maxwell-Boltzmann theory.

The theory contained the explanation of Brownian motion.

We can't see the molecules as they move and collide, but if we have a body small enough to be kicked around by them, and large enough to be visible in the microscope, we see "Brownian motion". That it was first observed in water was an accident, but the explanation is the same.

But we still have not answered the earlier question of how many gas molecules are there in a given volume. It was Joseph Loschmidt (1821-1895), also of the University of Vienna, who tackled the problem. Publication of his results took the form of a lecture delivered during the Twenty-Second Session of the Imperial Academy of Science in Vienna on October 12, 1865. The lecture had the somewhat surprising title: "On the Size of Air Molecules". Loschmidt explained that he used this term because the difference in weight of oxygen and nitrogen molecules is minor, so that they could be averaged to hypothetical air molecules. Now, he said, we are dealing with three values. One is the number of molecules per cubic centimeter—this we'll call N. Then we have the length of the mean free path, which we'll call L. And finally we have the diameter of the molecule which we'll call *D*. *L* will be shorter as the values for *N* and for *D* become larger.

So far everything was quite clear. If the number of molecules per unit volume is larger, there will be more collisions. But there will also be more collisions if the molecules themselves are larger. Hence his main interest was in the size of the molecules; all else would follow from that.

Maxwell had calculated that the mean free path for a nitrogen molecule would be (at 15° centigrade) 1/447,000 inch, equivalent to 6/100,000 millimeter. (We now know that the value is around 9/100,000 millimeter.) Loschmidt thought that Maxwell's figure was a bit too small so he picked 14/100,000 which is too large.

So each moving molecule moves through a volume of space which is cylindrical with the length of the cylinder being *L*, or Maxwell's "corrected" figure, while the diameter of this cylinder is equal to the still unknown diameter *D* of the molecule.

Trying to determine *D*, Loschmidt assumed that the molecules in a liquefied gas touch each other. This was quite a simplification, and even if the molecules were strictly spherical and touched each other there would still be 26 per cent of the total volume that would be empty.

Just to complicate matters, it was still impossible to liquefy air at the time Loschmidt lectured. Hence he could not know the volume occupied by one gram of liquefied air. He assumed a value by comparison with those gases that could be liquefied in his day.

He concluded that the diameter of an air molecule was just slightly less, by three per cent, than one millionth of a millimeter. This, he said, was not a correct value but he felt sure that it was "neither ten times too large nor ten times too small." In that he was correct; his value was only three times too large.

Strangely enough he did not take the step to calculate the

number of molecules in a cubic centimeter of air, but following his method that figure comes out as 1,800,000,000,000,-000,000 per cubic centimeter. But Loschmidt had overestimated both the size of the molecule and the length of the mean free path; the true number of molecules per cubic centimeter is 15 times as large.

Usually this is called Avogadro's number. In order to honor Loschmidt for his pioneering effort the number of molecules *per mol* (the quantity of compound weighing as many grams as its molecular weight, or 32 grams in the case of oxygen) is called "Loschmidt's number", although he did not calculate it.

That writers, even of textbooks, sometimes call Loschmidt's number Avogadro's number is sad, but true. Just console yourself with the thought that "gas" means "chaos"!

13

The Sound of the Meteors

ON APRIL 25, 1966, a very bright meteor flashed across the sky over the northeastern states. I am sorry to say that I missed seeing it. But several professional astronomers did see it and they estimated the altitude as about 35 miles. One newspaper reporter who saw it too wrote a fine report in which he remarked that what impressed him most about the fiery display was its complete silence.

Since the altitude was over 30 miles it would have been miraculous if there had been any sound. But while this particular case is simple and clear-cut there have been many occasions where chance observers of large meteors did report sounds, following immediately or very soon after the flash in the sky. In some cases the sound was compared to a pistol shot, in others to a volley of rifle shots; one observer said that his particular meteor made a sound like that produced by tearing stiff paper. Most observers compared it to plain thunder.

Did they report correctly, or did they ascribe chance sounds produced by something else at what they considered to be the right time to the meteor that was actually soundless?

I once worked with a man whose favorite conclusion was: "at this point we need a mathematical analysis." It became a catch phrase around the laboratory for two reasons. One, it did not matter too much what was under discussion to make him ask for a mathematical analysis and, two, he never made that analysis himself but assigned it to whoever was within reach and not obviously busy with something else. But at this point I have to call for a mathematical analysis myself . . . but I can assure the reader that it will be simple.

Meteors heat up when they enter the earth's atmosphere because they move so fast that the air in their flight path cannot get out of the way and is compressed, just as if that air were enclosed in a cylinder and the moving meteorite were the piston. Of course, some of the heat generated by this compression is transferred to the meteorite, and at an altitude of 77-80 miles it has become hot enough to glow and to be visible. The altitude at which the glow becomes visible is almost unaffected by the size of the body. Only a rather massive meteorite, weighing twenty pounds or more, may penetrate to an altitude of, say, 60 miles before becoming visible. Having a larger mass it needs more time to be heated up to the necessary temperature.

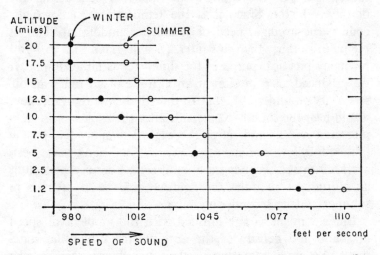

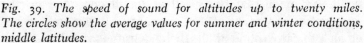

Fig. 39. The speed of sound for altitudes up to twenty miles. The circles show the average values for summer and winter conditions, middle latitudes.

The typical shooting stars, cosmic dust grains, become visible when they are 80 miles up and usually disappear at an altitude of about 55 miles. By then they have been consumed completely. The larger ones—with an original weight of ½ an ounce or so—will penetrate to about 40 or even 30 miles above the ground before they are consumed. The large ones with an original weight of a pound or more will actually reach the ground.

Having stated the observed facts about meteors, the next step is to have a look at the speed of sound.

Regardless of what many people think—and even regardless of what they may have been taught by teachers who were not up to date—the speed of sound in air does not depend on the density of the air but only on its temperature. In warm air sound travels faster. The difference between sea level air and stratospheric air amounts to almost precisely 100 miles per hour. It is because sea level air is denser than stratospheric air that the mistake was made of considering the density a factor. Since it is the temperature that actually counts, the average speed of sound, for middle latitudes, is higher in summer than in winter. (See diagram, Fig. 39.) But for many practical purposes the difference is rather minor. If we produced an explosion at an altitude of 20 miles an observer at "ground zero", that is, directly below the explosion, would hear the sound 104 seconds after the explosion in summer, and 108 seconds after the explosion in winter. In the table to follow summer and winter conditions have been averaged to 106 seconds for ground zero. For an explosion at an altitude of 10 miles the figures would be 51 seconds in summer and 53 seconds in winter.

But we are not quite finished with the problem of speed of sound and density of the atmosphere. When the statement was made that the speed of sound depended on the temperature it was, of course, assumed that the air is dense enough to carry sound at all. If the density is very low, which means that the molecules are rather far apart, you no longer get any sound waves, even with an explosion that would be rather noisy in denser air. In our atmosphere this is the case for any altitude above 25 miles. Meteors, then, can produce sound effects only below 25 miles. Of course this calculation

TABLE

Time to Ground in seconds
(rounded off to nearest half second)

Altitude above ground in miles	90°	45°	30°
20	106	148.5	212
17.5	92	129	184
15	79	110.5	158
12.5	65	91	130
10	52	73	104
7.5	39	54.5	78
5	25	35	50
2.5	12	17	24
1.2	6	8.5	12

contains a few assumed values that might be slightly different in reality; some experts therefore put the limit at 22 miles instead of 25.* To be safe let us deal with a maximum altitude of 20 miles only.

It is now quite easy to calculate how much time will go by between a noise-producing event at a certain altitude and the arrival of the sound on the ground. The table gives the results. In the column marked 90°, it is assumed that the observer is directly below the noise source. But in reality this would be a rare event. The line from the noise source to

* The density of the Martian atmosphere at ground level was found by *Mariner IV* to be only 1 per cent of sea level density on earth. The ground level density of the Martian atmosphere, therefore, corresponds to our atmosphere at an altitude of 19-20 miles. The Martian atmosphere is barely capable of carrying sound, but the noise of an explosion at the surface would be carried by the ground too.

the observer may form an angle of 45° with the ground; or the noise source might be even closer to the horizon, say at an elevation of only 30°. The table also gives the times for these two slant ranges.

As can be seen from the table, the sound produced by a meteor at an altitude of 20 miles and 30° above the horizon will need about 3½ minutes to reach the observer. An explosion 10 miles above the ground and 45° above the horizon will be heard on the ground after a minute and 13 seconds. It is therefore very likely that an observer, even if he does hear the sound produced by a high meteor, will not connect the two events. Being used to the idea that thunder follows lightning within a few seconds he will connect any chance noise that occurs within 4 or 5 seconds with the meteor.

But this does not mean that each and every report of noise produced by a meteor was the result of a mistake in judgment. There are a few famous cases where there can be no doubt.

Early in May, 1803, a report that numerous stones had fallen from the sky reached the Academy of Sciences in Paris. Up to then the Academy had been very skeptical about such stories and had tended to deplore them rather than to investigate them. But only a few years earlier Ernst Friedrich Florens Chladni had published a report on stones and irons that in all probability had fallen from the sky that had made an impression on a number of members of the Academy. So it was decided to send a younger member of the Academy, Jean Baptiste Biot, to the place where the phenomenon had been observed. It was the small town of L'Aigle in the Departement de L'Orne, 80 miles west of Paris.

Biot first established the time. It had been 1 P.M. local time on the 26th day of April 1803. The sky had been clear except for one small cloud. Loud sounds like explosions had been heard for a period of 5 to 6 minutes; everybody agreed that they came from above and since this cloud was the only cloud in the sky it seemed to be the logical source of the noise. Immediately afterward 2000 stones were seen to fall. The largest that was found weighed 18.7 pounds, but most were smaller; the smallest pieces collected weighed less than half an ounce. Biot noted that stones could be found only in an elliptical area one hour's journey in width and about 2½ hours' journey in length. Biot referred to the time it took to walk across and along the area; about 3 by 8 miles.

Since the cloud produced by the explosion of the meteorite cannot have been very large, it probably was less than three miles from the ground to be visible and the noise would reach the ground in 12-15 seconds. This time it was nearly vertically overhead. That the noise was actually produced by the exploding meteorite cannot be doubted, the only doubtful statement is that the explosions lasted "from 5 to 6 minutes". This seems too long by several minutes, but might be explained by putting the statements of different observers at different slant ranges together. They each heard the same set of explosions but at slightly different times.

Another famous old case is the meteorite of Ensis-Heim, in Alsace. It was actually seen to fall, between 11 A.M. and noon on November 19, 1492, and eyewitnesses said that there was a loud crash of thunder and a prolonged noise from afar, a description that sounds very much like what we now know as sonic boom. It made a hole five feet in depth, was dug up and weighed—260 pounds—and then taken to the village church. It so happened that King Maximilian I was there at the time. He ordered the stone to be brought to his castle where he knocked off two pieces, one to send to Duke Sigismund of Austria and one for himself. Then he ordered the stone to be preserved without further damage in the church. After a long time it was moved to the City Hall; at any event it was preserved for centuries.

At that time there already existed a forerunner of the newspapers of a later date. Bibliophiles know this forerunner

under the name of *Einblattdruck,* a German term meaning
one-sheet-print. An *Einblattdruck* was printed when a special
event was to be reported; a large percentage of them deal
with comets and the "meaning" of the appearance of one.
But this event also rated an *Einblattdruck.*

To round off this short survey the most recent major fall
of meteorites must be mentioned. It is known as the Sikhote-
Alin meteorite fall after the name of the mountain range in
eastern Siberia where the impact took place. The date was
February 12, 1947, and the local time was 10:38 A.M. The
sky was cloudless.

Professor E. Krinov of the Soviet Academy of Sciences
described the event as follows: "A scintillating ball of fire
with a luminous tail and sparks sped for several seconds
across the cloudless sky in broad daylight. The bolide was so
bright that it blinded the eyes of people watching it and it
cast moving shadows. In its wake there remained a wide gray
band of dust that was seen for several hours. Some minutes
after the fireball disappeared powerful detonations were
heard, resembling explosions or the firing of heavy guns."

The actual impact point was quickly spotted from the air
because the area was still covered with snow; the places where
the fragments of the meteorite had hit looked brownish as
they do in summer. Expeditions set out from both Vladivostok and Khabarocsk for a preliminary survey. They found
over 120 impact craters ranging in size from 1½ feet to 90 feet
and 78 holes less than 1½ feet in diameter that had been
produced by the fragments. Fragments could be found everywhere. Some fragments had struck trees so that the angle
of impact could be established directly. The gray dust that
had hovered in the air after the passage of the body had settled in the meantime and was partly recovered from the
ground with the aid of powerful magnets. It proved to consist
of round globules of iron that had formed in midair. Some

of them had fused together and most of them could be seen only with a strong magnifying glass.

It could be calculated later on that the meteorite must have entered our atmosphere with a relative velocity of 8.7 miles per second. The original weight must have been on the order of 30 tons. The pieces sent to Moscow for examination had a total weight of 23 (metric) tons. The investigation of these pieces not only gave the chemical composition (93.5 per cent iron; 5.27 per cent nickel; 0.47 per cent cobalt; 0.20 per cent phosphorus and 0.06 per cent sulfur) but it also showed why this meteorite had broken up as thoroughly as it had. It was not a homogeneous mass of meteoric iron but instead consisted of pieces that seem to have been fused together by pressure or heat sometime in the distant past. Moreover the iron parts were often separated by thin layers of a mineral called schreibersite which is a compound of iron and phosphorus. These mineral layers provided natural lines of cleavage. Presumably the meteorite had already broken apart during the passage through the air. The larger fragments that might still have weighed a ton or more then broke apart when they struck the rocky ground.

I have selected these three cases of meteoric noise because they represent three different types of noise production. The noise heard over L'Aigle was, in all probability, produced by the breakup of the meteorite after it had traversed the upper layers of the atmosphere more or less in one piece. It is unfortunate that we know nothing of the angle of the flightpath in this case; the stones that fell from the cloud fell vertically or very nearly so and obviously with subsonic speeds.

In the case of the older fall in Alsace the description sounds as if the meteorite reached the ground intact, having traveled with supersonic speed almost until impact. What the people heard was the noise of the impact and then the sonic boom produced earlier.

The Siberian meteorite of 1947 must have moved with subsonic speed by the time it became visible because nothing that could be ascribed to a sonic boom is mentioned. The sound resembling the noise of artillery fire that was heard was caused by the not quite simultaneous impacts of many fragments. If the sky had been cloudy at the time the impact noises would have produced a prolonged thunderous roar because of the reflection of the sound waves from clouds at different heights.

And now we can sum up the whole problem of noises produced by meteors.

Fig. 40. *Sketch map of the area of the 1947 Meteorite Fall. The distance of the impact point from Vladivostok is about 200 miles.*

If the noise-producing event—e.g., the breakup of the meteorite—takes place above 22 (or 25) miles nothing will be heard because no sound waves can be produced. If a bright meteor passes overhead at a height of less than 20 miles with an impact point a long distance away, a kind of faint thunder might be heard, but more than a minute after the phenomenon has been seen. This is the situation when mistakes are most likely to be made, with random noises ascribed to the meteor and its real noise being disregarded.

But an observer situated only a few miles from the impact point of a large meteorite might hear all three kinds of noise: the "boom" of the supersonic passage through the atmosphere, the noise of the breakup if it occurs and finally the sound of the impact.

14

Who'll Own the Planets?

IF CUSTOMS AND ATTITUDES had not changed during the last few centuries, this is what would happen on the day after a ship lands on Mars:

—If the name of the ship were *Miguel de Cervantes Saavedra* and that of the captain Don Francisco de Quintana y Molino, there would be a procession with banners of the cross around the landing site, two masses would be said, and in conclusion of the ceremony, a cross would be erected . . .

—If the name of the ship were *Dom Henrique* and the name of the captain João Dias, there would be the erection of a cross, a mass would be said and, in conclusion, a monument with a coat of arms would be placed . . .

—If the name of the ship were *Ilya Murometz* and that of the captain Vladimir Ossipovitch Kosmodemyanski, there would be a religious ceremony culminating in the ceremonial burying of copper shields with a coat of arms . . .

—If the name of the ship were *Queen Elizabeth* and that of the captain Sir Cecil Hawkins, there would be a brisk service and the captain would perform the "turf and sprig" ceremony, taking a handful of soil and any small plant in reach to take home with him. Then the British flag would be hoisted . . .

—And if the name of the ship were *Siegfried*, commanded by Captain Wolfgang von Greiffenklau, there would be an even brisker service. Then everybody would stand at attention while the German flag was being hoisted. Possibly the captain would stick his dress saber into the ground, or else (another tradition) pierce his own cap with it.

I don't know what would happen if the ship were named the *Robert H. Goddard* and the captain, F. Warren Smith, for all the customs mentioned had gone out of use at the time the thirteen states decided to be independent. But these were the actual customs for taking possession of an island or a coast.

Needless to say, none of these ceremonies would carry any legal validity nowadays and the International Court at The Hague wouldn't pay the slightest attention to even the most elaborate ceremony if the participants therein pack up and blast off for home at a later date.

The law. . . . Now just a moment. There is no space law yet, is there? The answer to that question is a clear "no" if you mean "legislation" when you say "law." As Rear Admiral Chester Ward said in a lecture on space law during the eleventh annual meeting of the American Rocket Society in November, 1956: "It is a fundamental principle of lawmaking that you can't legislate without facts. That principle applies just as well to the law of space as it does to the law that governs our actions here on the surface of the earth."

Since there are no "facts" yet—that is to say, no true spaceships with known performance characteristics and, by implication, performance restrictions—there can be no legislation.

But just because there are no such "facts" yet, the term "law" may be employed to mean what would otherwise be called a legal principle or a legal attitude. And that certainly exists. I have listened to about half a dozen lectures on the foundations and principles of space law during the last half dozen years—they were not evenly spaced, though—and found enough agreement between the various experts to make a résumé possible.

The earliest dissertation on space law saw print in 1932.

Its title was just that: "The Law of Space," but in German *Das Weltraum-Recht* and it was written by a Dr. Vladimir Mandl, who was then a practicing lawyer in Pilsen, Czechoslovakia. I freely admit that I hadn't looked at it since 1932 when Dr. Mandl sent me a copy and I have just read it to see what he had to say then.

Well, the net yield was tiny, for Dr. Mandl devoted most of his small book to investigating such legal problems as liability for accidental damage, etc., etc., and all that with special reference to German law. But he did say that space outside the atmosphere should be regarded as an area without existing or possible sovereignty, a point on which all later legal writers fully agreed.

The idea is very simply that open space is compared to the open sea. That no nation has, or can have, sovereignty over the open sea is a legal principle that has been firmly established for centuries.

We tend to think this is so obvious that it need not be mentioned, but there was a time—best nailed down as the time in which Columbus lived—when countries and even cities claimed ownership and sovereignty over oceans.

The Republic of Venice said it owned the Adriatic Sea. The city of Genoa countered this by owning the Ligurian Sea. Portugal claimed the Indian Ocean and the South Atlantic as hers, while Spain was content to own the Pacific Ocean (and the Gulf of Mexico). And the only reason that the Hanseatic League never said it owned the North Sea and the Baltic was that England, Norway and Denmark would have put in claims for the North Sea, too, and Denmark, Sweden and the countries of the eastern Baltic might have had strong opinions about the sole proprietorship of the Baltic.

Crowding sometimes has useful aspects.

Argument that the high seas should be free for the lawful use of all was first presented by the Dutch jurist Grotius, who is universally recognized as the "Father of International Law." But the fact that no nation, or organization of countries like the United Nations, has sovereignty over the high seas certainly does not make every ocean a lawless place. It developed its own law, based on practices which navigators found either efficient or convenient, and which were later formulated.

The statement that the laws which govern the sea should be extended to apply to interplanetary space was voiced—for the first time, as far as I know—by Oscar Schachter, deputy director of the Legal Department of the United Nations, on the occasion of the First Space Travel Symposium at the Hayden Planetarium in New York City in October, 1951 —appropriately enough, on Columbus Day.

But in order to gain the open sea, you have to traverse coastal waters, and in order to gain open space, you have to traverse the atmosphere. As regards coastal waters, the legal situation is clear; the problems were thrashed out and settled a century ago. The first three miles of ocean are considered to be under the sovereignty of the country which exercises sovereignty over the shoreline.

It has often been said that this figure of three miles was accepted because that used to be the range of the old coastal batteries. This sounded like a logical and convincing reason. Unfortunately, one could draw the conclusion from it that things belong to you for as far as you can shoot. That kind of reasoning would lead to declaring that "might is right" even legally.

Personally, I never quite believed that the three-mile zone had been derived from the range of the coastal guns, because a three-mile range did not become possible until many years after the limit had been accepted. And recently I learned that "three miles" was just a more modern way of expressing an older measurement, namely, one marine league.

There is something else about this three-mile zone which strikes me as either odd or significant—I don't know which. If what follows should be just a coincidence, it is a rare one.

There is a simplified formula which says you multiply the square root of h by 1.17 and you get D. The letter h stands for elevation above sea level and must be expressed in fact. The result D must be read in nautical miles and gives you the distance of the horizon at sea. If you take h to be six feet, the result is three miles (not nautical miles).

In other words, the three-mile limit coincides with the actual distance of the horizon for a man standing at the seashore. Remember that his feet will not be at actual sea level but a few inches above it. The refraction in the atmosphere is included in that conversion factor of 1.17.

To return to the legal aspects: most countries have accepted the three-mile limit and the United States recognizes no other, although there are a few countries which, for their own purposes (such as prosecution of smuggling), claim sovereignty over a longer distance, usually ten kilometers.

But while the countries "own" that much of the ocean, their ownership is not absolutely exclusive. There are exceptions. If a vessel, in order to pass from one tract of open sea to another one, has to navigate through sovereign waters, it can do so—it has the right of "innocent passage." (Whether naval vessels, in time of peace, have the right of innocent passage is disputed, but in time of peace, this problem is usually circumvented by prior agreement.)

When lawyers say "innocent passage," they usually mean freighters and passenger liners, but it also applies to rescue missions or scientific expeditions.

Now we come to the main difficulty. It would be nice if one could reason that, since space is analogous to the open sea, the atmosphere is analogous to the three-mile zone, with the right of innocent passage for all. If we had had peace ever since the invention of the airplane, one probably would reason that way. But there are two complications, each one major.

The first is the very obvious right of self-defense, and there are more military aircraft than passenger liners and air freighters.

The second is that no figure has so far been universally accepted as the limit of the atmosphere.

When you ask a scientist what seems to be a simple question, "How deep is the atmosphere?" he will look somewhat unhappy, draw a deep breath, stall by lighting a pipe, cigar or cigarette and say: "What characteristics do you have in mind?" The problem is that you still get some effects, like the reflection of short radio waves, several hundred miles up. On the other hand, you won't find noticeable air resistance, even at speeds of several miles per second, above 120 miles.

A few years ago, in a discussion of this difficulty, a law expert said that the *legal* limit might be determined by the height at which one can actually fly. Unfortunately I could not help him there. Jets and other air-breathing engines won't be able to go higher than, say, 70,000 feet.

But a large plastic balloon can go to 125,000 feet and a rocket-propelled plane still higher. Whether these "fly" or not is purely a question of definition. Is "flying" just moving through a space which still contains a little atmosphere, or is the term restricted to those altitudes where you still obtain some aerodynamic "lift"?

This, too, remains to be decided.

Our next step in disentangling the legal problem is obviously to find out what is the "law" in the air, the air in which we are now flying if we want to get from one city to another in comfort and with dispatch. Here the situation is sad, partly because of past experiences, partly because of old aspects.

The Romans held that the landowner also owned the air above it "to the sky." This idea was perpetuated in English common law, which said (still in Latin): *Cujus est solum ejus est usque ad coelum,* which later was expressed in English as: "He who owns the soil, or surface of the ground, owns, or has an exclusive right to, everything which is upon or above it to an indefinite height." (I don't know what practical importance that had, except when it came to the ownership of a bird shot on the wing.)

This personal and private ownership of the air and the sky above it was granted by the sovereign and "could be asserted only against other private citizens; the sovereign never parted with its paramount right to control the space above its territory." (Quotation from Andrew G. Haley's lecture *Basic Concepts of Space Law,* presented at the Annual Meeting of the American Rocket Society in Chicago in November, 1955; published in the society's journal *Jet Propulsion,* November issue, 1956.) In short, the attitude was the same as with the oceans.

As long as there was no human flight at all, or, at a later date, merely an occasional balloon, there was no legislation about the air. Lawyers say: *Minima non curat praetor,* which one may translate as: "Minor matters do not concern legislators." Not only was there no legislation, there was not even any theoretical reasoning.

The invention of the airplane changed this; in fact, one man was actually ahead of events. In 1902, at a meeting of the Institute of International Law, an expert named Paul Fauchille submitted a draft of a proposed convention on the regulation of aerial navigation. According to Haley, this draft was approved in a modified form in 1906.

Said Haley: "The convention would have made the air free to commerce and travel, just as the sea. The provision for national security measures, while vague and indeterminate, was a reasonable reservation of sovereign rights to protect against civil negligence or hostile action through the air, but it was not intended that any nation should usurp the air completely. The proposal was never implemented in an international convention."

I presume that it was still a case of *minima non curat praetor* with the few airships and planes which were around. At any event, nobody thought of prosecuting Blériot when he flew the English Channel and, so to speak, violated English air space.

But then the First World War came and it was one of the neutrals (generally a peaceful country in recent centuries) which had to defend vigorously the idea of sovereignty over its air space. This was Holland, lying as it does directly on the air route between England and Germany.

Of course there were violations. A couple of German zeppelin airships drifted off course in foggy weather (zeppelin ships, as a matter of principle, hid in drifting clouds to avoid being spotted, a method that may protect you but does not improve your navigation) and partly disabled seaplanes had to land in Dutch waters.

Right after the First World War, in October, 1919, the Paris Convention for the Regulation of Air Navigation was signed and "freedom of the air" was completely ruined in the very first article of this convention: *Les Hautes Parties Contractantes reconnaissant, que chaque Puissance a la souveraineté complète et exclusive sur l'espace atmosphérique au-dessus de son territoire;* "The High Contracting Parties recognize that every Power has complete and exclusive sovereignty over the air space above its territory."

Note the "complete and exclusive," and, of course, this included sovereignty over the three miles of ocean offshore. In practice, this complete and exclusive sovereignty was somewhat limited by rules of conduct.

The rules established, on the one hand, the right of innocent passage for non-military aircraft, and, on the other hand, the right to set up "prohibited zones" which could not be flown over. But—and this turned out to be the worst feature in the long run—these rights applied only to those countries that signed the convention. Nations which were signatories had the right to make separate agreements with nations which were not, but in reality they mostly refused to make such agreements and spent their energy in keeping the non-signatories out.

As for the United States, its representatives signed the convention with the provision that American aircraft could fly over American "prohibited zones." But the Senate did not ratify the convention, so the United States ceased to be a signatory. However, we observed the rules just the same and finally made a general Western Hemisphere right-of-innocent-passage agreement.

There was a welter of additional conferences dealing with all kinds of side issues—such as cases of infectious disease discovered on an international flight—and then the Second World War came. Again each nation, and most especially the neutrals, had to assert all their rights vigorously.

Near the end of the war, another important convention on civil aviation took place, this time in Chicago. It ended in December, 1944, but again the main article read the same, almost word for word, as the first article of the Paris convention. Something new had been added, however: "No aircraft capable of being flown without a pilot shall be flown without a pilot over the territory of a contracting state without special authorization by that state." This was the first recognition of the existence of guided missiles.

The possibilities and capabilities of aerial warfare being what they are, it is both natural and logical that every nation insist on absolute sovereignty over its "air space." The real trouble is that there is no definition of what is "air" in the term "air space." Since there is no natural upper limit to the height at which "aircraft capable of being flown without a pilot" (read: missiles) can fly, one might argue that there is no upper limit to the "air space." In the light of astronomical facts, this argument is plain nonsense.

As C. Wilfried Jenks of the International Labor Office in Geneva wrote in the *International and Comparative Law Quarterly* (January, 1956):

> "Any projection of territorial sovereignty into space beyond the atmosphere would be inconsistent with the basic astronomical facts. The rotation of the earth on its own axis, its revolution around the sun, and the motions of the sun and the planets through the galaxy all require that the relationship of particular sovereignties on the surface of the earth to space beyond the atmosphere is never constant for the smallest conceivable fraction of time. Such a projection into space of sovereignties based on particular areas of the earth's surface would give us a series of adjacent irregularly shaped cones with a constantly changing content. Celestial bodies would move in and out of these cones all the time. In these circumstances, the concept of a space cone of sovereignty is a meaningless and dangerous abstraction."

Admiral Ward, in his recent lecture, after saying in different words what I just quoted from Jenks, could indicate a way out:

> "Professor Cooper, and other distinguished authorities, have pointed out that our development of a law of outer space is not restricted by our present agreements affirming each nation's sovereignty over the air, or the 'air space,' above it. These agreements relate strictly to the 'air space.' They apply only as far as the upper limits of the region in which air is sufficiently dense to support the flight of conventional aircraft—that is, those aircraft supported through reaction with the air. We are therefore free to develop a law of outer space, to apply in areas above this region of relatively dense air, without restriction from our existing agreements relating to 'air space.' The lawmakers wait only for the physical facts of space to be supplied by the explorers, the scientists, the mathematicians and the physicists. With the physical facts in hand, we can attempt to set the upper limits of national sovereignty."

Admiral Ward went on to state that such an upper limit of sovereignty would not hamper national defense. The three-mile limit also does not hamper our naval operations and other defense measures at sea.

Let us say now that agreements have been reached, signed and ratified which set the upper limit of the "air space" at 50 kilometers, which is almost precisely 31 miles. Then we would get the following picture:

Up to a height of 31 miles, each nation has the "complete and exclusive sovereignty" first accepted in the Paris convention. Above that, there would be a zone with the right of innocent passage. For scientific reasons, this zone should not be lumped with "open space," because some physical phenomena due to a highly attenuated atmosphere can still be observed.

Open space may then be said to begin at a height of 250 kilometers or 155 miles (I am putting kilometers first because, by Act of Congress, the customary American standard measurements are defined in terms of metric measurements), so that there are three legal zones.

The bottom zone, with its complete and exclusive sovereignty, would *not* compare to the three-mile zone but rather to rivers and inland lakes. The next zone, from 50 to 250 kilometers, would be comparable to the three-mile zone. And space above 250 kilometers would be comparable (better: analogous) to the high seas.

But there is still an amusing wrinkle—these three zones would logically be in existence *only* above land. They would not exist for three-quarters of the Earth's surface, for over the high seas, the freedom of the seas would extend into space with no legal zone in between. Or else you may say that the freedom of space would end where your ship gets wet with salt water. Then you are in the free and open seas.

Legal discussions may be interesting, but how does all this apply to the satellite shots? By an interesting combination of natural facts, these satellite shots happen to be about as "legal" as they can possibly be.

The satellite boosters are fired from Cape Kennedy in Florida. American-made, they take off from American soil and, for a time to be measured in seconds, they are in American air space above American waters. When they leave American air space, they are in the free air over the free ocean. By the time land is below again (the southern part of Africa), they have passed out of any air space and are in free space.

Now how about that ship that lands on Mars and its captain who takes possession with or without ceremonies? In the first place, it is possible—even probable—that an agreement might be reached in the meantime that all "land" beyond the earth will be under the jurisdiction of the United Nations, unless inhabited by indigenous intelligent and reasoning beings. (In the latter case, naturally, *they* would have sovereignty.) All rights, including mining rights, if any, would take the form of concessions, leases or licenses from the United Nations.

But suppose it is not a case of the United Nations—which really means nations acting together instead of separately—but still a case of separate nations, generally at peace. There are some interesting analogies in the past and I'll quote Bouvet Island as an example. It is a small island, situated several hundred nautical miles to the SSW of the southern tip of Africa. The island itself is roughly circular, with a diameter of about five miles measured east to west and about half a mile less measured north to south. It is essentially just one large dead volcano, completely covered with glaciers.

Bouvet Island was discovered in 1739 by the French captain Lozier Bouvet. He thought it was just a northern cape of a much larger southern continent and named it *Cap de la Circoncision*. He made no legal claims. Since the area where the island is located is also characterized by the worst climatic conditions possible—frequent storms, long-lasting fogs, drifting ice—the island was "lost" for many years.

It was found again by the English captain James Lindsay in 1808. He tried to land but could not; by sailing around it, however, he established that it was an island. In December, 1825, the English ship *Sprightly* under Captain George Norris found the island, sailed around it, and Captain Norris took possession of it (from shipboard) for the United Kingdom in the name of King George IV.

There followed another period of uncertainty whether the island existed at all, but in November, 1898, the German oceanographic expedition with the steamer *Valdivia* found it again. The Germans decided that landing would be very difficult and would not accomplish anything anyway, so they did their charting and mapping from aboard their comfortable steamer. And although they named the largest glacier they could see the *Kaiser Wilhelm Glacier*, they had no aspirations as to ownership. They were merely establishing the precise location and size of this British possession.

But in December, 1927, the Norwegian vessel *Norvegia* under Captain Axel Hornvedt reached Bouvet Island. A landing party went ashore and took formal possession for Norway in the name of King Haakon VII. England objected, pointing to its Captain Norris. England lost the dispute, for the men of the *Norvegia* had actually landed.

But it cannot be denied that Norway's title to the island, acquired in 1928, is none too solid. They did land, which was deemed more important than prior discovery from a distance. But they have never *exercised* their sovereignty. And this has come to be an important point; if somebody else sneaked in during the antarctic night and established a colony, he might win out over Norway, since Norway has obviously been negligent in asserting its rights by possession.

The history of Bouvet Island may, in the future, become famous because of citations in legal arguments. In the meantime, it indicates that nobody will be able to "own" a planet by just saying so.

If mere discovery established ownership, then the naked-eye planets—Mercury, Venus, Mars, Jupiter and Saturn— would be common property. They were discovered by the Babylonians who left no heirs and assigns. Our moon would be community property, too.

Otherwise, Germany and England would fare best, with the largest chunks of celestial real estate: Germany could claim Neptune and England Uranus. But Uranus was discovered by Herschel, who was German-born, and though he made the discovery from English soil, he may not yet have been an English citizen at that moment, which would produce an interesting legal problem.

The Netherlands would get Titan, Saturn's largest moon. Italy would get the four largest moons of Jupiter and possibly several of the smaller moons of Saturn, depending on whether their discoverer, Cassini, was still an Italian or already a Frenchman when he found them.

England, in addition to Uranus, would get all the four large moons of that planet, the larger moon of Neptune and two of the minor satellites of Saturn. The United States would get the two moons of Mars, a handful of the minor moons of Jupiter, one minor moon of Saturn, the smallest moon of Uranus, the smaller of the two moons of Neptune and the planet Pluto. Of course, practically all of us would "own" at least a few asteroids.

But remember, discovery by itself does not count. You've got to land on your asteroid—and stay there—to make it legal.

15

Death of the Sun

ONE OF THE FIRST BOOKS I ever bought—a mixture of curiosity and nostalgia caused me to buy another copy some ten years ago, my first having been lost—was a small volume by the German astronomer, M. Wilhelm Meyer, called *World's End*. It was paperbound, with a melancholy cover painting which carried out the theme. There a small group of emaciated humans huddled in the snow near a dead tree, and low in the sky was an enormous deep-red sun.

It was the same basic idea which had been painted with words by H. G. Wells in his *Time Machine*. You probably remember the story: After having seen and experienced the end of the human race on a trip into the future, the Time Traveler lets his machine race far, far ahead. At first, there is the "blinking succession of day and night" to which he has grown accustomed during earlier time trips, but as the machine continues into the future, things slowly change:

"The band of light that had indicated the sun had long since disappeared; for the sun had ceased to set—it simply rose and fell in the west, and grew ever broader and more red. All trace of the moon had vanished. The circling of the stars, growing slower and slower, had given place to creeping points of light. At last, some time before I stopped, the sun, red and very large, halted motionless upon the horizon, a vast dome glowing with a dull heat, and now and then suffering a momentary extinction. At one time it had for a little while glowed more brilliantly again, but it speedily reverted to its sullen red heat. I perceived by this slowing down of its rising and setting that the work of the tidal drag was done. The earth had come to rest with one face to the sun . . ."

If I saw this old German painting or read the *Time Machine* for the first time now, I could date both painting and story from this one fact. Both would have to fall into the period from roughly 1880 to 1900, because of this dying red sun which looks so much larger because the Earth has moved closer to it along the tight spiral of a steadily shrinking orbit. Actually, the story was written in 1895 and the picture was painted in 1903—only ten years later, the writer would have been doubtful and the painter would have picked something else from the book.

The very question of whether the Sun might one day die was still relatively new when Wells actually wrote, strange as that may seem to us. It had been the subject of doubtful speculation and worried calculations for only a few decades. In earlier days, that question simply did not exist and we don't even have to go back to the time of Homer when the Sun was the chariot of the sun-god to find it lacking. While people had thought about the end of the "world" on and off in olden days, the possible end of the Sun had never been considered.

None of the Greek philosophers concerned themselves with this problem. The Roman writers had far more mundane things to consider. The Bible even stated, by implication, the opposite: "while the earth remaineth . . . summer and winter, and day and night shall not cease."

Nor did the astronomical revolution started by Nicholas Copernicus change the picture. What *did* begin to change the attitude was not philosophical ideas, but facts which were uncovered because of the spare-time activities of one Jan Lippershey in the Netherlands, which resulted in the invention of the telescope. In December, 1610, it was found for the first time that the Sun was literally not spotless.

The man who usually is credited with the discovery of the Sun spots is the pastor David Fabricius, but part of the credit should go to his son Johannes, for father and son worked together in observing the skies with their recently acquired "optick tube." Johannes, in fact, saw it first.

The Sun, he wrote later, did not look as clear and smooth as he had expected. "It seemed to have various kinds of roughnesses and unevennesses, even at the rim. As I watched carefully, an unexpected darkish spot showed itself, not at all small as compared to the size of the Sun. I thought that drifting clouds caused the spot."

Even after reassuring himself "about ten times" that the spot could not be a cloud, "I did not trust myself completely and called my father . . ." The father-and-son team not only discovered the Sun spots, but, by observing them, the rotation of the Sun.

Before David Fabricius had published the findings, a Jesuit priest, Father Christoph Scheiner, in Ingolstadt, saw several Sun spots. As required by his order, Scheiner reported his find to his superior Buseaeus, who listened carefully, thought for a while and said: "My son, I have read all the writings of Aristotle several times from beginning to end and can assure you that I found nothing in them which says what you tell. Go and calm yourself; be assured that what you believe to be spots in the Sun are flaws of your glasses or your eyes."*

The Sun's corona was discovered, too, as soon as a suitable

* This is not quite as bad as what was done some 45 years later. Christian Huyghens in the Netherlands had invented a new method for grinding and polishing lens. He built himself a telescope and promptly discovered Titan, Saturn's largest moon. He just as promptly discontinued his observations, reasoning that there were six planets (Mercury, Venus, Earth, Mars, Jupiter and Saturn) and now also six moons, that of Earth, the four of Jupiter discovered by Galilei and the one of Saturn he had discovered. Since the number of moons could not be larger than the number of planets, they obviously had all been found!

eclipse occurred. It was, of course, elementary knowledge even then that an eclipse was the result of the Moon moving across the line of sight from the Earth to the Sun. The question was which of the two was the possessor of the corona.

Around the year 1700, Giacomo Filippo Maraldi, a nephew of the great Jean Dominique Cassini, and famous as an astronomer in his own right, stated as his opinion that the corona was the atmosphere of the Sun which suddenly became visible during a total eclipse. But the majority of his colleagues considered it much more probable and "reasonable" that the corona was the atmosphere of the Moon, which was illuminated for good visibility only if the Sun stood directly behind it.

The question was solved by elimination: The more the Moon was observed, the clearer it became that the Moon did not have an atmosphere worth that name. Hence the corona had to belong to the Sun.

Yes, but what were the Sun spots?

Galileo Galilei believed they were black—or at least dark—clouds that were high above the luminous surface of the Sun. Others did not contradict this view, but were more specific—these were the dark clouds that formed above gigantic volcanoes in eruption.

A few decades later, about 1670, it was Cassini who turned the idea around. The Sun spots were not dark clouds of one kind or another, but just the opposite: When a storm tore a hole in the luminous cloud layers of the Sun, it might grow tenuous enough to be pierced by a vast black mountain peak on the Sun's surface.

That it might be the Sun's atmosphere which was luminous while the surface was dark was not Cassini's original idea. It had been uttered somewhat timidly at an earlier date by pointing out the highly luminous clouds we now call sunset cumulus and which are so much brighter than the ground. Cassini's authority merely reinforced this older idea.

A century later—things did not move as fast then as they do now—Cassini's special contribution to this theory was removed, but the theory itself seemed strengthened some more.

In November 1769, the Sun sported an especially large spot and Alexander Wilson in Glasgow, who observed it with meticulous care, realized for the first time what virtually everybody knows now from photographs. Such a Sun spot was not just a dark blot; it showed some differentiation in itself. The center was really dark, but between this dark spot and the surrounding bright surface of the Sun was a medium-dark area. When such a spot had wandered all the way to the rim, one could see that perspective made the relative positions of the dark center spot and the not-so-dark surrounding area shift.

In short, one could see that the semi-dark area was lower than the surrounding luminous area, while the dark center area was still lower.

Obviously, then, there were several layers in the Sun's atmosphere, one highly luminous top layer (but still below that ghostly corona one could not normally see) and a less luminous lower layer. Each layer developed holes on occasion and if the holes in both layers happened to match, we could see the dark "real surface" of the Sun.

Although Sir William Herschel held to the maxim that "it is sometimes of great use in natural philosophy to doubt of things which are commonly taken for granted," he wholeheartedly accepted Wilson's reasoning. He only made a minor correction: Wilson had spoken of the "lower layer" as less luminous, whereas Sir William considered it to be dark. We could see it at all only because of the fact that it reflected the light of the higher luminous layer.

In the elder Herschel's opinion, the surface of the Sun was *protected* against the heat and glare of the top layer by this reflecting and absorbing lower layer. To bolster the idea that all the luminousness might originate only from the Sun's

upper atmosphere, Sir William pointed out that all heavenly
bodies, "we have pretty good reason to believe, emit light
in some degree." The dark side of the Moon did so on occasion—actually reflected Earthlight which is reflected sunlight in the first place—the night side of Venus often glowed
(probably aurora) and, in the polar night of the Earth there
was the glowing *aurora borealis* in the north and the equally
bright *aurora australis* in the south.

It was a difference in degree rather than a fundamental
difference. "The sun's similarity," Sir William wrote in 1794,
"to the other globes of the solar system with regard to its
solidity, its atmosphere and its diversified surface; the rotation upon its axis, and the fall of heavy bodies, lead us on to
suppose that it is also most probably inhabited, like the rest
of the planets, by beings whose organs are adapted to the
peculiar circumstances of that vast globe."

We would be hard put nowadays to invent anything wilder
than this concept, but it covered all the then available information. As long as not even the nature of chemical com-
bustion was properly understood, it made sense.

To us, it seems like an especially striking contrast that
Herschel, with such a concept in mind, also tried to establish
whether the Sun spots influenced the weather on Earth.
Having neither astronomical nor meteorological statistics
available, he picked the only one there was—the recorded
wholesale prices of grain. Even so, he might—with luck—have
discovered the Sun-spot cycle, but the tool was too inade-
quate.

The actual discovery of the Sun-spot cycle by Heinrich
Samuel Schwabe did not take place until 1843, but around
1770, a Danish astronomer had resolutely entered a remark
in his daily diary to the effect that "in time, a periodicity
of the Sun-spot phenomenon will be found, since every other
astronomical phenomenon shows periodicity."

Herschel's concept of the Sun was not disproved by one man and one discovery at a specific date. It seems to have died very gradually, its last remnants being swept away by the discovery of spectrum analysis in 1859.

In the meantime, a large number of other discoveries had been made and some known phenomena had been thought about. By 1840, no astronomer doubted any more that all the so-called fixed stars were suns, too—as had been guessed by an Arab eight centuries earlier—and the phenomenon of the Milky Way had been explained, by Herschel as a result of observation, and by Immanuel Kant independently by careful reasoning. One of the discoveries that became important was that some stars showed definite colors. That some were red was obvious, but there also were blue ones.

So stars could have different colors—at that time, it was just an item of information to be filed away.

Then there were the recurrent "new stars." Pliny the Elder reported that Hipparchos had started his famous star catalogue because of such a new star. You could not tell whether a star was "new" if you did not have a list of the "old" ones.

Two or three other new stars had been reported from Roman times. Then there had been one during the ninth century when Arab astronomy was at its peak under Caliph al-Mamun. In 1012, Hepidanus, a monk of St. Gallen in Switzerland, listed another "new star" in his *Chronicle of Miracles*. One especially famous super-nova, to use the modern term, occurred in the time of Tycho Brahe (1572). Another one soon after, in 1604, has often been called Kepler's new star. Jean Dominique Cassini got "his" in 1670; then there was a pause until 1848.

Of course, there have been quite a number since, but the ones that influenced thinking in 1840 were those associated with the names of Brahe, Kepler and Cassini.

If stars could have different colors, would it be possible that there were *dark* stars? When Alexander von Humboldt wrote jokingly in a letter about such dark celestial ghosts, the then famous astronomer Friedrich Wilhelm Bessel (the first to measure the distance to a star, 61 Cygni) replied simply: "that innumerable stars are visible obviously does not disprove the existence of an equal number of invisible stars." So if there were dark stars and also "new" stars, wasn't the simplest explanation of the "new" stars that two dark stars had collided? Thus the novas seemed to furnish a roundabout proof for the existence of dark stars.

Such an event was both end and beginning, but the idea of "the end" had entered astronomical thinking, so to speak, by the back door. For what were the dark stars?

In 1814, Joseph Fraunhofer, discoverer of the lines named after him and *almost*-discoverer of spectrum analysis, had compared the lines of various stars. He had found that his lines were in places where the Sun did not show lines and had concluded that there probably were different kinds of stars.

Fraunhofer's discovery had come clearly too early to be fully understood. It took until 1860, when Giovanni Batista Donati came across Fraunhofer's statement in an old volume of the proceedings of the Munich Academy of Sciences. Donati himself went to work on the problem, but most of the work was done by Father Angelo Secchi, the Papal Astronomer.

Angelo Secchi sorted all the stars he investigated into four classes. Class I were the "blue stars" of which Sirius and Vega are examples. Class II were the "yellow stars" with our own sun as the prime example. Class III were the "red and orange stars," such as Betelgeuse and alpha in Hercules. Class IV, finally, was a type of which very few and very small stars were then known. They were dark red and their spectrum was strange.

Such stars, Father Secchi wrote, "which show such zones

in their spectra must have a lower temperature than those which show only the fine lines (of Fraunhofer)." In fact, the explanation seemed to be that the stars of Class I and Class II were far too hot to permit the existence of chemical compounds, while the stars of Class III and especially of Class IV were not hot enough to prevent their existence.

We now know that this is wrong, but the consequences of this careful pioneer work were very obvious: Secchi's four classes were clearly four successive stages of a star. Or a sun. At first, it began hot, blue-white. In the course of time, it cooled to yellow. Then to orange. Then to red. In the end, it was too cool to be visible at all—Bessel's dark stars.

So far, everything looked logical and fine. The stumbling block appeared with the logical enquiry of how long this development would take. It was the same question as "what keeps the Sun going?" There were estimates of how much heat the Sun produced. We know that these estimates were too small, but they appeared enormous.

John Tyndall (a physicist, not an astronomer) said in despair, "the facts are so extraordinary that the soberest hypothesis must appear wild." The Sun kept everything going on Earth, as had been well realized by then, but the Earth intercepted only a tiny fraction of the Sun's production of heat and light. Any reasonably bright high-school boy, knowing the diameters of the Sun and the Earth and the distance between them, could calculate just how much radiation the Earth intercepted. The figure is on the order of 1/2,200,000,-000.

A few scientists (but not physicists), both astonished and somewhat frightened by such figures, tried to think a way out. Maybe the Sun did *not* radiate into space in all directions. Maybe radiation between the Sun and the planets was a proposition resembling static electricity—it went only in the direction in which it was received.

This was a somehow valiant guess, utterly wrong, of course, and promptly disbelieved by every expert, even before James Clerk Maxwell's *Treatise on Electricity and Magnetism* in 1873 furnished the final demolishing weapon.

The fact remained that the Sun threw enormous amounts of energy into space. Where did it come from?

Sir William Thomson, the later Lord Kelvin, made a quick side calculation. Even if the Sun consisted of the best grade of anthracite and were furnished with the necessary oxygen, it would not last more than 5000 years, so it could not possibly be chemical energy. In the first place, it obviously wasn't. In the second place, geologists had already shown that the Earth was far older than 5000 years and that, moreover, there had been life on Earth for a very much longer period.

But what other energy than chemical energy was there? Here Hermann von Helmholtz had given an answer. The Sun must have had a beginning and the only possibility one could think of was that it had condensed out of cosmic dust. It must have been large and loose in the past, but the mutual gravitational attraction of the particles caused this body to condense into what we now call the Sun. Such contraction generates heat. Helmholtz advanced the theory, for the first time, in 1853, that the Sun kept going by continued contraction.

Calculation showed that a contraction of about 300 feet per year should account for the observed release of energy. And since, with contraction, its surface is diminished, it should actually grow hotter. Because the contraction would amount to one mile every 17 years and the diameter was 864,000 miles, however, the shrinkage would be too small to detect easily. It certainly could not be detected by comparing older records with modern (1860) observations.

Extrapolating backward from this idea, it turned out that the Sun could not be older—as a shining star—than 18 million years at the most. Simon Newcomb, extrapolating forward at a later date, calculated that after five million years, the Sun would have shrunk to half of its present diameter and be eight times as dense. After that, the ability to contract any more would be drastically reduced and the temperature would have to fall off sharply.

The overall conclusion was that the Sun would last another eight million years or so.

The maximum figure of 18 million years for the past was greeted with pleasure at first by the geologists, who found in their own researches that every new discovery they made needed more elapsed time. But the geologists kept on making discoveries and the figure of 18 million years soon grew tight for them.

Well, astronomers and physicists interested in astronomical matters were willing to oblige with an alternate idea. Lord Kelvin, who himself estimated the age of the Earth as about 100 million years, was in favor of the meteoritic theory, which claimed that the Sun maintained its heat by the impact heat of the steady rain of meteorites that must fall into it.

To get a grip on the problem, Lord Kelvin calculated how the solar furnace would be stoked by the impact of the planets it now has. If Mercury fell into the Sun, it would make up for the energy release of about 6½ years and Venus would account for nearly 84 years of energy release. The table looked as follows:

Mercury	6.6 years
Venus	83.8 "
Earth	95.0 "
Mars	12.6 "
Jupiter	32,254.0 "
Saturn	9,652.0 "
Uranus	1,610.0 "
Neptune	1,890.0 "
Total:	45,604.0 years

From this table, one could calculate back how much matter would have to fall into the Sun daily to keep the process continuous. The result happened to produce a nice even figure: If a mass equal to 1/365th of one per cent of the mass of the Earth fell into the Sun daily, it would account for the energy release. Rounded off: one Earth-mass per century. This would not show up as an increase of the diameter of the Sun for a long, long time.

If the geologists had balked at the contraction hypothesis because it did not allow them enough time in the past, the astronomers balked against the meteoritic hypothesis because it would put too much matter into space.

If the equivalent of one Earth-mass fell into the Sun every century, the equivalent of several Earth-masses—no, of scores of Earth-masses—must be in space reasonably near the Sun.

But the astronomers would see them. The Earth itself, for one thing, would find a heavy meteoritic bombardment going on all the time. The orbits of the inner planets would be influenced. It might work theoretically, but it did not agree with observed facts. It was like saying that the observed level of street noise at a busy intersection could be accounted for by pistols being fired at the rate of four rounds per second. The noise might be the same, but the bullets would cause other effects which, however, did not show up.

The majority of astronomers thought along a different path. The observed energy release of the Sun—facts first!—could be accounted for by either of these two theories. But either should have effects which disagreed with observation. Therefore, both probably worked together.

A steady hail of meteorites stoked the solar furnace, but there was not enough to replace all the lost heat. The difference was made up by contraction which, under these circumstances, could be much slower. Hence the geologists got more time in the past because of lesser contraction, while the observing astronomers were still not asked to accept larger amounts of cosmic matter than they would willingly do.

All this could be made to account for continued sunshine. But most likely there were elaborations. One could see the red suns in space. They had obviously run out of meteoric material and then contracted as far as possible, after which they only lost heat, with no chance of replenishing the supply, until their temperature had dropped to the point where chemical compounds became possible. Soon they would be completely dark.

But if they had planets, there would be respites, just as suggested by Lord Kelvin's calculations. The planets, moving around their suns, must find some slight resistance—infinitesimal, to be sure, but resistance nevertheless. Slowly, their orbits would shrink and finally one would crash. The sun would be rekindled—remember Wells: "had for a little time glowed more brilliantly again"—and then slowly disappear again in reddish blackness until the next planet crashed. Seen from a long distance, this would be one of the "new" stars.

This concept also explained the observed fact that these new stars did not last long. They suddenly flamed into enormous brilliance from "nothing," outshone everything else for months, but then became faint and could not be found any more after a few years. If they had been collisions between two dark stars, they should be permanent as far as short-lived humans were concerned. But a crash of a small planet seemed to fit the facts.

Extending speculation a bit, there were two schools of thought. Both agreed on the general scheme for quite a long way. A star formed somehow and, with the aid of meteoric material and contraction, it kept shining for a long time, until the meteoric material was used up and contraction, as higher densities were reached, became more difficult. Near the very end came the borrowed time of the planet crashes.

The question was—and here the two schools of thought differed from each other—what was likely to happen if you did not look at one sun, but at all of them together—at the Galaxy, as it were?

One party maintained that the average number of luminous stars would remain substantially the same because of collisions of dark stars and the "original formation" of new ones. The other group maintained that the number of luminous stars must decrease steadily, for there was no "original material" left to form new stars and every pair of dark stars that met would make just one new, though larger, luminous star.

Therefore, after eons and eons of time, all the matter would be concentrated into just two supergigantic stars. Alone in space, they would, of course, attract each other and these two would suffer a head-on collision of enormous masses striking at fantastic speed.

This unimaginable collision could not produce a single star. It would disperse the matter of both!

But the end of one cycle would be the beginning of the next, for then there would be again matter in space, to condense and form completely new stars and planets and moons!

The picture was complete around 1890.

In 1896, the professor of the *Ecole Polytechnique*, Antoine Henri Becquerel, put uranium ores into the same desk drawer in which he kept unexposed photographic plates, wrapped in black paper. Two years later, Pierre and Marie Curie isolated something they called polonium.

That the atom was not strictly indivisible and that energy was released by this very fact became known during the decade from 1896-1906. Some ten years after that, Sir Arthur Eddington began his theoretical work on stellar interiors. At almost every point of his thinking, lack of knowledge of atomic behavior interfered and he finally exclaimed that he had intended to delve into the interior of the stars and ended up in the interior of the atom. But this apparently irrelevant detour actually cleared up the question.

We must keep in mind at this point that up to the year 1919, it was believed that radioactivity could not be influenced in any way. It had been found in the laboratory that certain heavy elements—uranium, polonium, thorium and radium—did "decay" into something else, releasing energy in the process. But the decay rate seemed to be given and fixed. It remained the same in the coldest cold chamber that could be produced. It did not change with heat. It remained uninfluenced by electric currents or magnetic fields.

In 1919, Ernest Rutherford succeeded in smashing a nitrogen atom. This opened entirely new vistas. One had not been able to influence radioactivity by heat or by electric currents. Maybe it merely had not been hot enough or the current had not been powerful enough.

Ten years after Rutherford, two young scientists, Robert Atkinson and Fritz Houtermans, dared to say for the first time that the nucleus of an atom might be attacked if it was hot enough. As is now known, the kinetic energy of a bit of matter increases with heat. The hotter it is, the faster it will move and the energy, naturally, depends on the speed.

When Atkinson and Houtermans made their statement, it was a comparatively recent item of knowledge that under conditions of extreme heat, something else will happen to atoms. Normally, which in this case means any temperature from room temperature to that of molten steel and beyond, each atomic nucleus is surrounded by its swirl of electrons.

Simplifying things a bit, it was assumed that these electrons had a kind of cushioning effect. If, at "normal" temperatures, one atom bumped into another, they bounced off their electron shells, the nuclei remaining unaffected. But as the temperature went up, the electrons were gradually "stripped" from the nucleus; at very high temperatures, the nucleus of the atoms would be bare. At the same time, the speed with which they moved was increased by the temperature, too.

Then, in a stellar interior, you had "naked nuclei" racing about at colossal speeds.

Under these conditions, it seemed possible—even probable —that the nuclei might be affected by collisions. But that was as far as one could go in 1929—the general statement that "thermonuclear reactions" *should* be possible was all that could be said. One could not yet be specific.

If you read popular articles on atomic energy nowadays, you can easily get the impression that it all began with the accidental discovery of the fission of uranium by Hahn and Strassman. And that, after this discovery had been verified and the fission bomb had been built and used, scientists began to wonder about the fusion of light atoms and finally contrived the hydrogen bomb.

Now this may be a nice and simple scheme for explaining things to an outsider, but it is not correct historically. Even before it was known that heavy elements like uranium could go into fission, scientists were talking about generating atomic energy by fusion. Not that they talked about doing it themselves; they talked about it as something that probably went on inside the stars.

One likely reaction seemed to be the fusion of a lithium nucleus and a hydrogen nucleus into a helium nucleus. But that could not be what happened in our sun. It would be far too fast under the circumstances actually prevailing. It would result in one big flash and that couldn't be it. As George Gamow wrote then, "We know, therefore, that our sun cannot contain any appreciable amount of lithium in its interior, just as we know that a slowly burning barrel surely cannot contain any gunpowder."

What really keeps the Sun going was figured out for the first time under somewhat unusual circumstances. In 1938, a Conference on Theoretical Physics took place in Washington, D. C., and one of the participants was Dr. Hans Bethe of Cornell. As he was riding home on the train, he decided that one should be able to find the proper reaction by checking through a number of possibilities. It seemed likely that the energy output of different nuclear reactions should differ greatly in magnitude so that, if one could find a nuclear reaction which tallied with the actual energy release of the Sun, one could be fairly sure of having the right one.

Professor Bethe started checking through a number of likely nuclear reactions. Before his train pulled in, he found one which gave the right result!

Strangely enough, Dr. Bethe's colleague, Karl von Weizsäcker in Germany, arrived at the same result (I don't know under what external circumstances) at the same time. The cycle of reactions is usually called the "Solar Phoenix Reaction" because the carbon atom which is involved reappears unchanged at the end, so that it acts more like a nuclear catalyst.

Naturally, in such a self-consuming cauldron as the Sun, with the enormous size and the temperatures involved, more than one nuclear reaction will go on. A little over 10 per cent of the total energy generation is thought to be due to what has been called Critchfield's H-H process which assumed a head-on collision of two protons (hydrogen nuclei) with subsequent ejection of a positron. A third reaction that probably happens is this one.

(Table 1)

THE SOLAR PHOENIX REACTION

Step No.	Reaction	Time Constant for Center of Sun
(1)	$_1H^1 + {_6}C^{12} \rightarrow {_7}N^{13}$	40,000 years
(2)	$_7N^{13} \rightarrow {_6}C^{13} +$ positron	10 minutes
(3)	$_6C^{13} + {_1}H^1 \rightarrow {_7}N^{14}$	7,000 years
(4)	$_7N^{14} + {_1}H^1 \rightarrow {_8}O^{15}$	1 million years
(5)	$_8O^{15} \rightarrow {_7}N^{15} +$ positron	2 minutes
(6)	$_7N^{15} + {_1}H^1 \rightarrow {_6}C^{12} + {_2}He^4$	20 years

Net result: $4\ {_1}H^1 \rightarrow {_2}He^4 + 2$ positrons

As has been intimated, the various thermonuclear reactions depend on temperature. Obviously they cannot be the same for every star; some stars are hotter than our sun and some are cooler. In a star like Sirius—hotter but otherwise of the same general type—there can be very little of the H-H process, while this process might be the sole or at least main energy source in a fainter star.

Knowing now that thermonuclear reactions—fusions of light atoms—provide the energy of the stars and knowing, too, at what temperature the various reactions can take place, we can search an entirely new picture of stellar evolution.

You remember what they thought of stellar evolution before atomic energy was known. In the beginning, they put an uncondensed star—the term now in use for this is "proto-star"—which by way of contraction was finally hot enough

(Table II)
POSSIBLY "COMPETING" REACTION

Step No.	Reaction	Time Constant for Center of Sun
(1)	$_1H^1 + {}_1H^1 \rightarrow {}_1H^2 +$ positron	10^{11} years
(2)	$_1H^2 + {}_1H^1 \rightarrow {}_2He^3$	2 seconds
(3)	$_2He^3 + {}_2He^4 \rightarrow {}_4Be^7$	30 million years
(4)	$_4Be^7 +$ electron $\rightarrow {}_3Li^7$	1 year
(5)	$_3Li^7 + {}_1H^1 \rightarrow 2\ {}_2He^4$	1 minute

Net result: $4\ {}_1H^1 + 1$ electron $\rightarrow {}_2He^4 + 1$ positron

to shine with visible light. As contraction progressed, the star went through a white phase (Sirius as an example) then through a yellow phase (our sun as an example) and finally, when most of the energy had been radiated away but contraction was virtually finished, the red phase. The black and invisible phase was to be the end.

The modern concept still begins with the proto-star, a fantastically tenuous accumulation of gas molecules with some cosmic dust mixed in; that dust later evaporates into gases when the temperature rises. And early in the career of a star, old Helmholtz's contraction theory actually applies to the full.

The heat generated is produced by contraction and, as the process goes on, the star grows hotter, producing more heat by contraction than is radiated away from its steadily shrinking surface. Therefore the temperature in the core approaches a point, after a while, where thermonuclear reactions will start. At that time the star is still enormous as far as volume occupied is concerned, but is still very tenuous and not very luminous. It is a so-called Red Giant.

Taking a specific Red Giant, epsilon Aurigae, it can be demonstrated that the temperature of its core is not yet high enough to keep a reaction of the type of the Solar Phoenix cycle going. The reaction must be between deuterium and hydrogen (or heavy hydrogen and ordinary hydrogen), resulting in helium and energy.

It is an interesting point that the star's mass acts as a kind of safety valve. Supposing the nuclear reaction was too violent, the heat produced would simply expand the whole star. That way, the radiating surface increases and, in an extreme case, the core may simply grow too cool to sustain the nuclear reaction. Then the star would rely on contraction until the core grows hot enough again.

Astronomers know a number of stars which bear the designation of "pulsating stars." They expand and shrink at regular intervals. It is thought—but, as far as I know, not yet completely proved—that these pulsating stars are forever on the borderline between Helmholtz's contraction and thermonuclear energy generation.

Every time they have contracted enough to heat their interior to nuclear activity, the nuclear activity grows violent enough to expand the whole star and quench the nuclear fire. Just what conditions are necessary to put a star into this dilemma is not yet known. Obviously the majority of the stars somehow escaped this difficulty and went on to higher core temperatures. Some known Red Giants must rely on the lithium-hydrogen reaction mentioned earlier. Still hotter ones rely on a reaction converting boron and hydrogen into helium.

You must have noticed that these thermonuclear reactions which keep the stars going always end up with helium. Since the reactions must start at the very core, where it is hottest, one can assume that helium will accumulate at the core, finally to the virtual exclusion of all other atoms. Logically then, as a star grows older, the reaction no longer takes place at the precise core. That is taken up by the atomic slag heap of helium atoms.

We have to picture, in that case, a core of no longer reacting helium, of uniform and very high temperature. The "surface" of this central helium sphere is where the thermonuclear reactions take place. The area above the reacting spherical shell is still too cool to let reactions take place. As this reacting sphere grows, the rate of conversion of other elements into helium grows, too. Hence as a star uses up its fuel faster, the less is left of it.

Percentagewise, Sirius "burns up" more hydrogen atoms than the Sun every second. It is, from this point of view, an "older star" while our sun is still so young that its end lies not several million but several billion years in the future.

At some time near the end of the star's life, something happens. Possibly the generating shell comes so close to the surface that all the nuclear fuel above it is consumed in a flash. After that, the star collapses to form one of the superdense White Dwarfs. Since a White Dwarf has absolutely no method of energy generation left—it has used up all the elements which could be nuclear fuel and cannot contract any more—it must be considered "dead."

As a side-issue, I would like to mention a recent idea about the Blue-white Giants. Fred Hoyle in England has made much of the idea of stars passing through clouds of cosmic dust and acquiring large amounts of matter by "tunneling" through such a dust cloud, a variation of the old meteoric impact theory. Such an event must be rare, but astrophysicists feel that the rare Blue-white Giants fit this assumption. They are, then, not stars in a certain (and somewhat mysterious) state of stellar evolution, but "rejuvenated stars" which might have held any place in stellar evolution before they entered a cloud.

How about the "black stars," though, which were so much discussed a century ago? The overwhelming probability is that there aren't any. As long as there is *any* method of energy generation left, the star will utilize it. And when it has finally reached the ultimate stage of the White Dwarf, it combines an enormous heat content with a very small radiating surface, since a collapsed star probably has about the same diameter as the Earth.

Figuring things very carefully, a White Dwarf should need some 8000 million years to radiate away its energy and turn dark.

The question "When will the Sun die?" is, in terms of that fact, just about as academic as any could be. If it's keeping you up nights, you have about 4000 million years—minimum! —to stay awake worrying, so let's put out the light and go to sleep, shall we?

16

The Re-Designed Solar System

AT ONE TIME IN MY CAREER—it was in summer, 1929—I was
asked to write an introductory article for a special issue of a
German movie magazine. That special issue was for the pre-
miere of the first large scale space-travel movie, Fritz Lang's
Girl in the Moon. Having worked myself into a poetical mood
by thinking of the past and of the future simultaneously, I
conceived the idea of the "three eras of astronomy".

During the first, the pre-telescopic era, astronomers could
only determine the positions of the fixed stars in the sky and
the movements of the planets among them. They could neither hope to find the sizes of the planets—if, indeed, they
differed in size—nor could they expect to find out any of the
distances.

Then came the second era, that of the telescope. It first
proved that the planets were solid bodies, it made it clear
that they were of different sizes, it established their distances
and finally it even found the distances to some of the nearer
fixed stars. But then the question of the surface conditions
on the various planets came up, and the most determined
efforts with the telescope, and later with spectroscope and
camera, only produced "educated guesses" and speculation.
It was rarely possible to draw a line between the two. Therefore I wrote that the second era had succeeded in solving all
the unsolved problems of the first era—but had created a
number of problems of its own.

Ah, but the third era, the era of space-going devices! That third era would solve all the problems posed by the second era. More in the spirit of tolerance than out of conviction, I added that the third era might pose some problems of its own.

Well, we are in the early stages of that third era by now. Some problems that were inherently insoluble for the second era, like the appearance of the far side of the moon, have been nicely solved. Quite a number of other things have happened too, and, taking refuge in that half sentence that "the third era *might* pose problems of its own", I can say that I foresaw this fact.

But I did not expect new problems to crop up right at the outset of the space age. Nor did I expect that space age astronomy would re-design the whole inner solar system. As far as the inner portion of the solar system is concerned, literally every member of it, including our own Earth, has been changed around.

Let us begin with the planet nearest the sun, Mercury.

Mercury has always been a "difficult object", to use the cautious language of the astronomer. At the very best the angular distance of Mercury from the sun is 27 degrees and 45 minutes of arc. That means that, as seen from the Earth, Mercury is always close to the sun. It can therefore only be seen in a sky that is illuminated by the sun, either at dusk or at dawn. And, of course, you have to have a horizon that is free of clouds and haze. It is an interesting fact that Nicholas Copernicus knew of the existence of Mercury only second-hand; late in life he complained that he had never seen it himself.

Yet the light coming from Mercury, even though it is only reflected sunlight, is by no means weak. If we could have Mercury in the midnight sky it would outshine Sirius. It is the proximity to the sun that causes all the problems.

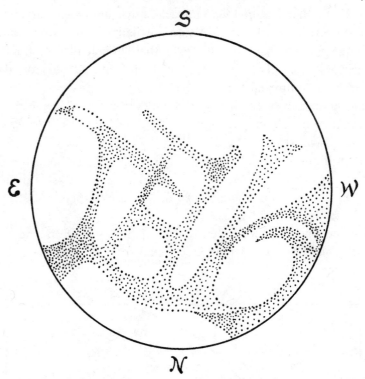

Fig. 41. *The Bright side of Mercury as drawn by G. V. Schiaparelli and later by E. M. Antoniadi.*

At one time the Italian astronomer Giovanni Virginio Schiaparelli decided that one could gain a little by observing Mercury in daylight. Of course the sky would be still brighter, but at least the planet would be high in the sky so that our atmosphere would not be so much in the way. The idea proved to be so useful that in 1893 Schiaparelli could announce—with the King and Queen of Italy in the audience, no less—that Mercury had a period of rotation that matched its period of revolution, hence that it always turned the same face to the sun, just as the moon does with earth.

With that lecture, the concept of Mercury that survived until last year was born. Not quite half of the planet was never reached by the sun's rays; there the leftovers of the original atmosphere would be lying frozen on the ground. And not quite half of the planet's surface was ever under the fierce rays of the nearby sun, and tin and lead, if present, would form shimmering puddles on the hot rock. Between these two extremes there was the promise-crammed Twilight Belt, illuminated but hardly heated by slanting sunlight for a few days of every Mercurian year that lasts only 88 days. This concept was fine and logical and firmly established for threescore and ten years.

And then what happened? Then they started bouncing radar impulses off Mercury and found that Mercury is slowly turning on its axis.

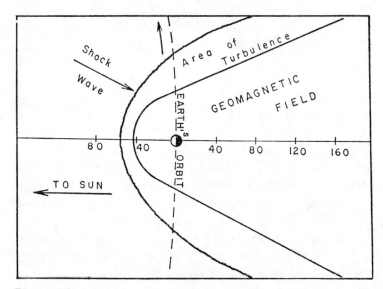

Fig. 42. The beginning of the earth's "magnetic tail." The figures give distances in thousands of miles, measured from the center of the earth.

Its year is still 88 days, but its day is only about 64 days. The result, of course, is that both the sunlit side and the dark side wander slowly around the planet. The sunlit side will still be very hot, but it will get a chance to cool off. And the dark side will become the sunlit side at regular intervals— which means that there can be no remnants of the Mercurian atmosphere left. All the gases that might have existed there once must have escaped into space a long time ago.

While I was contemplating the problem of how to re-write the section on Mercury in my *Conquest of Space,* a reader sent me something that was labeled "an unpoetic fragment", with permission to quote but with simultaneous insistence on "no screen credits, please!" The Mercury section reads:

> *Gone the thrilling tales of Brightside*
> *Neatly paired with chilling Nightside*
> *Not even now a Twilight Zone,*
> *The darn thing rotates, just like home.*

But I feel obliged to add that "home is still a thousand times more comfortable"—at least to us.

Well, the discovery of the rotation of Mercury may have destroyed a few cherished concepts, but after all this is progress. Didn't space age astronomy neatly solve the problem of Mercury? Well, yes, but . . .

But there is the problem of some pictures.

Schiaparelli, when at the height of his career, drew a chart of the brightside of Mercury (Fig. 41). Some fifteen years later the Greek-born French astronomer Eugenios-Marie Antoniadi also drew a chart of the brightside of the planet. Except for the fact that Antoniadi filled in some areas, like the oval on the lower right of the drawing, with a uniform gray shade, the two drawings are alike.

But if Mercury rotates, how can this be explained?

Well, there is a possible explanation, and it has to do with what Percival Lowell termed a "presentation". When observ-

ing Mars, Lowell had to keep in mind that the rotation of
Mars is a bit slower than that of the earth. If you had a certain
view of Mars at 10 P.M. on a given night, that same view
would not occur at 10 P.M. the following night, but at about
10:40 P.M. Then you had the same view in the telescope—
the same "presentation". Now Schiaparelli's drawing shows
one specific presentation of Mercury. Antoniadi's drawing is
evidently the same presentation.

But why are there no other drawings of other presenta-
tions, since Mercury rotates? If one assumes that the other
hemisphere of Mercury is devoid of outstanding features and
therefore looks just like a blur, these two drawings can be
reconciled with a rotation: they both would show the only
"presentation" *where something can be seen.*

If anybody should tell me that this is merely an excuse I
made up in a hurry I would have to accept the accusation.
We'll simply have to wait and see what additional work will
turn up. In the meantime this explanation has to serve—
because there is no other.

Progressing to the next planet, Venus, the changes brought
about by space age astronomy are less disappointing—or more
so, depending on what you believed before. When I heard
my first lectures on astronomy I learned that there were two
views of Venus. One had the classical name of *panthalassa*
(meaning "all ocean") and according to this view Venus was
completely covered by water. There might be a few small
islands, but a large land mass could not exist. If there were
one, it would cause vertical currents in the atmosphere and
these currents would break up the uniform cloud layer which
every observer complained about.

The other view did admit land masses, but not dry land
masses. Land masses there might be, but everything would be
swampy, covered with shallow lakes. In a few elevated areas

there might be stretches of dripping jungle. And who could tell what weird animals might walk or crawl around in the eternal greenish dusk?

In the interval between the two world wars a third view of Venus was conceived. One could have the unbroken cloud layer, which was the main fact known about Venus, without endless oceans. One could have the same clouds if Venus were completely dry, with all the water in its atmosphere in the form of vapor, while on the ground, at a temperature above the boiling point of water, endless dust storms were raging. Space probe *Mariner II* showed that the surface temperature of Venus is 800 degrees Fahrenheit, so that the third view was proved to have been closest to the mark. Science-fiction writers realized that a whole shelf of nice Venus stories was suddenly obsolete, and my "unpoetic fragment" echoes their disappointment:

> *Bye-bye mermaids and dripping jungles*
> *Dinosaurs, large swamps and similar*
> *bungles,*
> *In fact, bye-bye Venus—you beautiful*
> *tease*
> *Till you explain those 800 degrees.*

As a matter of fact much more than those 800 degrees have to be explained. According to the findings of *Mariner II*, the atmospheric pressure at the ground must be ten to twenty times that of our atmosphere at sea level. The lower limit of the cloud layer would lie at about 15 miles, which is higher than the highest clouds (except for temporary volcanic clouds) in our own atmosphere. But the mass of Venus is about 81 per cent of the mass of our planet. How can Venus hold on to such an extensive atmosphere with a smaller mass —and, in addition to that, be closer to the Sun? Somebody should put a computer or two to work on that problem.

Progressing to the Earth, space age astronomy has not changed its surface, of course. But it has shown that the Earth has a number of things we have literally never seen.

Until airplanes climbed to high altitudes we had no idea of the existence of the so-called jetstream in our atmosphere. And until the first American satellite, *Explorer I*, climbed beyond 600 miles we had no idea of the radiation belt, now known as the Inner Van Allen Belt. When a friend of mine, a physicist, informed me of the discovery of the belt by long distance call from Washington and told me about the electrons and protons from the Sun that were trapped there by the Earth's magnetic field, I said something like: "One should have thought of that, shouldn't one?" and received the reply: "You and thirty-seven others!" Fact is that nobody did until it was discovered. Then everything was suddenly crystal clear and obvious.

Since then something else invisible has been discovered and it goes under the name of the "wake in the solar wind" or else the "magnetic tail". (Fig. 42) There is a steady stream of subatomic particles, mainly protons and electrons, leaving the Sun. This has been dubbed the solar wind. The Earth, with its pronounced magnetic field, must disturb the smooth flow of the solar wind, in the manner in which a rock in a shallow creek disturbs the flow of the water. The situation near Earth is shown in the diagram. As the solar wind encounters the Earth's magnetic field there is an interaction that has been labeled the shock wave. Just behind the shock wave there is an area of uncertainty; in some cases the Earth's magnetic field is more energetic than the particles of the solar wind, in other cases the particles are more energetic. But then comes the clear-cut superiority of the geomagnetic field which can be penetrated only by very energetic particles, so-called "cosmic rays". As shown in the diagram the geomagnetic field forms a spreading cone, pointing away from the Sun. But with increasing distance from the Earth the field must grow weaker and the particles of the solar wind more or less retain their energy. Hence at one point the area of disturbance in the solar wind must grow narrower and finally peter out. In short, the "magnetic tail" cannot be of indefinite length.

A few satellites specifically designed to investigate this question have been sent up. Originally they were designated IMP, for Interplanetary Monitoring Platform. Later the name was changed into Interplanetary Explorer Satellites. Unfortunately one of them did not attain the orbit into which it was supposed to go and therefore the measurements are incomplete. Most experts feel sure that the "magnetic tail" reaches beyond the orbit of the moon, but nobody can tell how far.

> *Electrons and protons by the bucket*
> *and gallon*
> *Produce the two belts named after*
> *Van Allen,*
> *But this moment the general wail*
> *Is: How long is our magnetic tail?*

Even in the case of the moon space age astronomy has produced a problem, in addition to providing a great deal of information. When astronomers were asked in the past about the probable appearance of the backside of the moon they would answer unanimously that there was no reason to suppose that the moon's farside would differ significantly from the side we can see from Earth.

A Russian rocket launched on "Sputnik Day"—October 4, 1959—succeeded in taking a few pictures that showed a portion of the moon's farside. The pictures were few in number, they were not very good, and the sole transmission of them that could be achieved was full of "snow". But what there was seemed to bear out the general idea: the backside of the moon looked generally like the visible side.

But on July 18, 1965, the Russians launched another space probe, dubbed *Zond III*. It passed the moon on July 20 at a distance of 7500 miles and took pictures for an hour and eight minutes. The Russians then waited until *Zond III* was quite some distance from the moon. On July 29 they sent the radio order to start transmission and a stream of pictures came back to the earth from a distance that had grown to 1,375,000 miles. They comprise a total of about three million square miles of the lunar surface, with much of it on the farside. These pictures are good and clear and they show that the moon's farside is marked up by a profusion of impact craters, just like the visible hemisphere. However they do not show any of the large gray *mare* plains which are visible with the naked eye.

Why our moon has *mare* plains on one hemisphere and not on the other—disregard the fact that one is the visible hemisphere and the other is not, that is probably accidental—is something that will need explanation at one time. At the moment it is one of the puzzles produced by space age astronomy.

And now we come to Mars.

On July 14, 1965, space probe *Mariner IV* passed the planet Mars after a flight from earth that had taken 228 days. The space probe was instrumented to take 22 pictures of the planet and everybody concerned had 7½ months during which to worry whether everything would go well. Could one rely on instruments that were exposed to space conditions for that length of time and that could not even be tested while underway? And somebody exacerbated the atmosphere by pointing out that the space probe might well collide with the inner moon of Mars, Phobos. Since one could not be sure of the precise hour of the fly-by and since Phobos needs only 7 hours and 39 minutes to complete one orbit around its planet one simply could not make sure of avoiding Phobos, especially since the closest approach to the planet was at about the distance of Phobos. In theory there was a safety margin of a few hundred miles, but no one could be sure that the course of the space probe would be that precise.

Well, Phobos was missed, the cameras functioned, *Mariner IV* disappeared behind Mars, measuring the density of its atmosphere in the process, and after it had reappeared the transmitter began sending the pictures to Earth, over a distance of more than 130 million miles. This had to be a point by point transmission because of the long distance, so it took about six hours for every picture to be completed by the transmitter.

The first of the pictures showed the rim of Mars and something next to it that could either be a high flying cloud or merely an imperfection in the system. But the next pictures brought a surprise; Mars looked like the moon in these pictures. There were large and apparently old craters, there were smaller and probably younger craters; it was simply and plainly a moonscape we saw.

I might say right here that this similarity was unduly enhanced by the fact that the pictures were in black and white. Seen through the telescope, Mars is the most colorful of all planets, with white polar caps, yellowish desert areas, dark areas that look gray or greenish, and an occasional white cloud, probably consisting of ice crystals. If the Mariner pictures had been in color they would not have looked quite as strange.

As the pictures progressed the areas photographed shrank in size (see table) so that the features showed up better. But it was always the same—craters, craters, craters. Pictures 9 and 10 should show a "canal" that can be seen on many maps.

THE MARINER PICTURES

Running number:	Center of picture in Martian		Slant range (miles)	Extent in miles	
	Latitude (degrees)	Longitude (degrees)		E. to W.	N. to S.
1.	+35	188	10,500	410	800
2.	+27	186	10,100	290	530
3.	+13	183	9,500	220	310
4.	+ 7	181	9,300	210	270
5.	− 2	179	8,900	190	220
6.	− 6	177	8,700	190	200
7.	−13	174	8,400	180	180
8.	−16	173	8,300	180	170
9.	−23	169	8,100	170	160
10.	−26	168	8,000	170	160
11.	−31	163	7,800	170	150
12.	−34	161	7,700	170	150
13.	−39	155	7,600	170	140
14.	−41	152	7,600	170	140
15.	−45	144	7,500	180	140
16.	−47	139	7,500	190	140
17.	−50	128	7,400	200	140
18.	−51	122	7,400	210	140
19.	−51	107	7,500	240	150
20.	focused on nightside of Mars, useless				
21.	same				
22.	same				

They didn't. Of course one could say that the time of the fly-by was the wrong season for Mars, a season where the "canals" always are weak. Or one might say that the space probe was so close, only about 8000 miles from the point to be photographed, that a canal would not show up because it would be lost among the detail photographed. Still, that leaves the question of just what is a canal as unanswered as it has always been.

That Mars should be covered with craters was, by itself,

not too surprising because of the vicinity of the planet to the asteroid belt. In fact it had even been predicted by an amateur, Donald Lee Cyr by name, more than fifteen years ago. But the overwhelming number of craters was still a surprise. It indicated that the craters were not worn down by erosion, and while it has always been agreed that Mars does not have much water, there had also been the agreement that it had *some* water, while these pictures looked as if it had none at all. There is a discrepancy here that will need explaining.

Now as the space probe went "behind" Mars there was a chance of measuring the density of the Martian atmosphere. The value obtained was much lower than anybody had expected. In the past the figure usually given was: pressure at ground level somewhat like ours 20,000 feet up. More recently, because of measurements and calculations by Gerard P. Kuyper, the answer was modified to read: like ours at 50,000 or 60,000 feet. But *Mariner IV* reported figures that made this like ours at 80,000 feet or even at 90,000 feet.

This, unfortunately, ruins the beautiful deep-blue sky Chesley Bonestell painted for my book *The Exploration of Mars* and my correspondent, with reference to these pictures, rhymed:

> *The Mariner fly-by has laid bare*
> *The little canal that wasn't there.*
> *Ditto skies of azure hue*
> *Chesley must be feeling blue.*

and concluded:

> *Quick, let's write about Saturn, Uranus,*
> *Jupiter*
> *Before science makes us feel stupider.*
> *Those cold facts, I'm trying to resist*
> *'em—*
> *Give me back my dear old Solar*
> *System!*

Well no, I can't bring the "old" solar system back, but I can point out that even the Mars measurements leave some room for doubt. So the pressure at ground level is now down to ten millibars. All right, measurements are measurements. But how about those dust storms that have been seen? Fig. 43 shows a drawing made by E. M. Antoniadi in 1909. At that

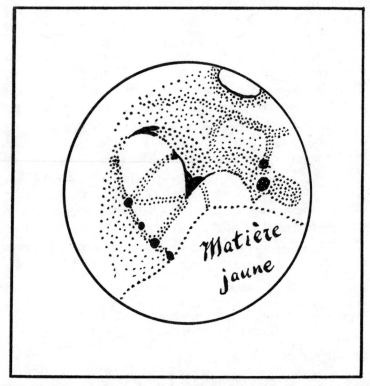

Fig. 43. Mars, as drawn by Antoniadi in 1909, showing a dust storm obscuring almost one quarter of the disk of the planet.

time the whole disk of Mars was hazy, but Antoniadi succeeded in making out the detail shown, except for an area of about one quarter of the visible surface where he left a blank space and wrote *matiere jaune* into it, "yellow matter". It was a dust storm obscuring an enormous area.

Does that tally well with a pressure of ten millibars?

I don't know the answer. All I can do is to sit back and trust to the proverb that time will tell!